SENTENCE COMBINATION
Writing and Combining Standard English Sentences

Book II

Alice C. Pack   Lynn E. Henrichsen

Brigham Young University
Hawaii Campus

Newbury House Publishers, Inc. / Rowley / Massachusetts / 01969
ROWLEY ● LONDON ● TOKYO
1980

Library of Congress Cataloging in Publication Data

Pack, Alice C
  Sentence combination.

  Continues the authors' Sentence construction.
  Bibliography: p.
  Includes index.
  SUMMARY: Explains ways to transform and combine
simple, error-free sentences into complex ones.
  1. English language--Study and teaching--Foreign
students. 2. English language--Sentences. 3. English
language--Rhetoric. [1. English Language--Sentences
2. English language--Rhetoric.] I. Henrichsen,
Lynn E., joint author. II. Title.
PE1128.A2P25   428.2'4'07   80-19416

Cover and book design by DIANA ESTERLY

NEWBURY HOUSE PUBLISHERS, Inc.

Language Science
Language Teaching
Language Learning

ROWLEY, MASSACHUSETTS 01969
ROWLEY • LONDON • TOKYO

Printed in the U.S.A.

First printing: January 1981

5

TABLE OF CONTENTS

The purpose of this book is to teach students who can already write error-free basic sentences to transform and combine such sentences into complex sentences of the types commonly used in edited writing—the type of expository prose generally expected in academic situations. The focus is on the sentence, although contextually connected exercises are used throughout the book.

Due to the contextualized nature of the exercises, the relationships between sentences are of critical importance. In addition to mastering the mechanics of sentence combining and transforming, students must recognize these relationships in order to successfully complete the assignments.

Students who are unable to produce error-free basic sentences should be referred to the appropriate sections in the companion volume to this book—*Sentence Construction*. Diagnostic materials for this purpose are provided in this text. To avoid confusion in referral to specific explanations and exercises after this diagnosis, the chapters in *Sentence Construction* are numbered one through eight, while those in this book begin with number nine.

Sentence Combination uses a step-by-step approach. Explicit instruction in combining methods eliminates the need for students to rely on intuition. Although the order of presentation used in the book—explanation, followed by examples, followed by practice—suggests a deductive approach to learning, this order can be modified by teachers who prefer to teach in an inductive manner, presenting examples first and then encouraging students to formulate rules before referring to the textual explanations.

All exercises are presented in sets of three (A, B, and C). In addition to providing substantial amounts of practice with each combining method, this feature allows the use of a spiral approach if desired. (The A exercises may be assigned in the first cycle, the B's used in the next, and the C's reserved for later use or review.)

After each combining method is presented and practiced, it is reinforced in the final exercises in subsequent chapters which require a cumulative knowledge of the combining methods presented to that point.

A NOTE ON SENTENCE COMBINING

Considerable research regarding the value of sentence combining in the classroom has been reported in recent years. Numerous studies have suggested that sentence-combining activities stimulate the development of syntactic maturity. Many successful teachers of writing have used sentence combining in various types of exercises with results as varied as the methods and techniques used.

Teachers who desire to learn more about experimental research involving sentence-combining, including its history, rationale, and current findings, are referred to the following bibliography:

Christensen, Frances. 1968. The problem of defining a mature style. *English Journal* 57: 572–579.

Combs, Warren E. 1976. Further effects of sentence-combining practice on writing ability. *Research in the Teaching of English* 10: 137–149.

Crymes, Ruth. 1971. The relation of study about language to language performance: with special reference to nominalization. *TESOL Quarterly* 5, 3: 217–230.

Daiker, Donald; Kerek, Andrew; and Morenberg, Max. 1978. Sentence-combining and syntactic maturity. *College Composition and Communication* 29, 1:36–41.

Daiker, Donald; Kerek, Andrew; and Morenberg, Max, eds. 1979. *Sentence Combining and the teaching of writing.* Akron: L & S Books. Univ. of Akron.

Endicott, Anthony L. 1973. A proposed scale for syntactic complexity. *Research in the Teaching of English* 7: 5–12.

Faigley, Lester L. 1979. Generative rhetoric as a way of increasing syntactic fluency. *College Composition and Communication* 30: 176–181.

Hunt, Kellogg W. 1966. Recent measures in syntactic development. *Elementary English* 43: 732–739. (Also in Lester, Mark, ed. 1973. *Readings in applied transformational grammar,* 2nd ed. New York: Holt, Rinehart and Winston.)

Hunt, Kellogg, W. 1967. How little sentences grow into big ones. In *New directions in elementary English,* ed. Alexander Frazier. Champaign: National Council of Teachers of English. (Also in Lester, Mark, ed. See Hunt, 1966 above.)

Hunt, Kellogg W. 1970. Do sentences in the second language grow like those in the first? *TESOL Quarterly* 4, 3: 195–202.

Hunt, Kellogg W. 1970. Syntactic maturity in schoolchildren and adults. *Monographs of the society for research in child development,* No. 134. Chicago: University of Chicago Press.

Hunt, Kellogg W. 1977. Early blooming and late blooming syntactic structures. In *Evaluating writing: describing, measuring, judging.* Champaign: National Council of Teachers of English.

Mellon, John. 1967. Transformational sentence combining: a method for enhancing the development of syntactic fluency in English composition. Final Report, Cooperative Research Project No. 5-8418, Office of English Education and Laboratory for Research in Instruction. Graduate School of Education, Harvard University, Cambridge, Massachusetts. (See also: Same title as above. *NCTE research report* #10. Champaign: National Council of Teachers of English.)

Morenberg, Max; Daiker, Donald; and Kerek, Andrew. 1978. Sentence combining at the college level: an experimental study. *Research in the Teaching of English* 12: 245–256.

O'Donnell, Roy C.; Griffin, William J.; and Norris, Raymond C. 1967. Syntax of kindergarten and elementary school children: a transformational analysis. *NCTE research report* #8. Champaign: National Council of Teachers of English.

O'Hare, Frank. 1973. Sentence combining: improving student writing without formal grammar. *NCTE research report* #15. Champaign: National Council of Teachers of English.

Shook, Ron. 1978. Sentence combining: a theory and two reviews. *TESL Reporter,* 11, 3: 4–7, 12, and 15.

Stevick, Earl. 1966. *A workbook in language teaching: with special reference to English as a foreign language.* New York: Abingdon Press, pp. 60–66.

Stotsky, Sandra L. 1975. Sentence-combining as a curricular activity: its effect on written language development and reading comprehension. *Research in the Teaching of English* 9: 30–71.

Strong, William. 1976. Sentence-combining: back to the basics and beyond. *English Journal* 65: 60–64.

Swan, M. Beverly. 1979. Sentence combining in college composition: interim measures and patterns. *Research in the Teaching of English* 13, 3: 217–224.

Weiser, Irwin. 1979. Sentence combining for diction and detail improvement. *Freshman English Resource Notes* 4, 3: 8–9 and 12.

STUDENT DIAGNOSIS AND REFERRAL

The following diagnostic materials may be useful to teachers who wish to use the individualized approach mentioned in the "To the Teacher" section of this book. As the first step in the student diagnosis and referral procedure, students write a short essay on a topic which calls for the use of different times, various forms of modifiers, comparison, transition, etc. Three example topics follow:

Write about your education. Where have you gone to school before? What are you studying now? When do you expect to finish? What are you going to do after that? How will you be different because of your educational experience?

Briefly describe your daily life when you were a young child and your daily life now. Then, explain the more important similarities and differences between them.

Write a description of something unusual that you have done recently or something unusual that has happened to you. Compare it with what you expected to do or expected to happen. Then tell what you expect to do in the future as a result of this unusual experience.

After students have written their essays, the instructor/tutor analyzes the errors and checks the appropriate categories on the diagnostic/referral checklist provided at the end of this section. The subheadings in each category may be circled to indicate specific problems.

The bracketed numbers following each category on the checklist refer to chapters in *Sentence Construction* and *Sentence Combination* which treat the particular problems listed in the category. (The *Dyad Learning Program* materials are separate Newbury House publications.) After diagnosis, students should be assigned work in the chapters/sections indicated on the checklist.

Other diagnostic methods and materials may also be used. A progressive diagnosis may be conducted by using one of the three assignments which follow each grammar explanation as a diagnostic exercise for the grammar point covered in that section. Other diagnostic materials, such as cloze passages keyed to specific errors (to facilitate referral), and/or sentence completion exercises which call for the use of a variety of grammatical constructions and times, may also be used. Examples of each follow:

Cloze Passage

For centuries men have wondered how man acquired or developed languages. Scholars still speculate on where [and] how man got his words. [One] linguist asserts that this has [occasioned] more interest and speculation, probably, [than] any other single aspect of [the] whole language problem. During the [eighteenth] and nineteenth centuries so much [attention] was addressed to this subject [that] the French Academy of Science [passed] a rule formally excluding any [more] communications on this topic from [its] transactions.

Theories of language origin [have] included the onomatopoetic or "bow-wow" [theory], or the idea that language [began] with imitations of sounds occurring [in] nature; the "ding-dong" theory, which [maintains] there is a mystic correlation [between] sound and meaning; the "pooh-pooh" [theory], which holds that speech first [consisted] of reactions to fear, pleasure, [pain], etc.; the "yo-he-ho" theory, which [asserts] that grunts from physical exertion [originated] language; and the "ta-ta" theory, [which] poses that vocal organs unconsciously [attempted] to mimic bodily actions or [mimic] gestures of the hands.

As [more] and more languages are analyzed [and] extensive information on language becomes [available], the faultier all these theories [that] language evolved from imitative sounds [or] primitive grunts and groans seem. Primitive languages are, as a rule, anything but primitive except with reference to modern civilization's vocabulary.

Exact word answers are given in brackets. Other contextually and grammatically appropriate responses should also be accepted. Incorrect responses should be analyzed and reported on the diagnostic/referral checklist.

Sentence Completion Exercise

Complete the sentences below. Make certain that your sentences are contextually connected in a meaningful way. In other words, write a story.

1. Some of my friends usually

2. While they do that, I sometimes

3. Although my mother

4. However, my father always   , and

5. Our neighbors have never

6. Every day they

7. Their children

8. Even their dog and cat

9. In the past, we

10. Now we only

11. In the future

As with the essay and cloze passage, student errors made in the sentence completion exercise should be analyzed using the categories on the diagnostic/referral checklist.

Diagnostic/Referral Checklist

WORD DERIVATIONS (forms of Content Words) [1]
    Noun, verb, adjective, and adverb form confusion/misuse

ARTICLES [2 and *Dyad Learning Program: Determiners*]
    Incorrect choice; unnecessarily used; omitted when needed

NOUNS [2]
    Singular-plural or count-noncount confusion/misuse; failure to use proper unit expression with noncount noun

PRONOUNS [3 and *Dyad Learning Program: Pronouns*]
    Lack of agreement with antecedent; ambiguous antecedent; no antecedent; unnecessarily used; not used when called for, incorrect form

AUXILIARIES AND MODALS (Aux-words) [4]
    Incorrect choice; omitted when needed; unnecessarily used

VERB FORMS [5, 7, and *Dyad Learning Program: Verb Forms and Verb Choices*]
    Incorrect form (base, *d-t-n*, *-ing*, *+s*, *no-s*, past); incorrect verb choice; unnecessarily used; omitted when needed; incorrect use of two-word verbs

VERB/AUX-AGREEMENT WITH SUBJECT (Harmony, Concord) [4, 5, 8:1 and *Dyad Learning Program: Verb Forms*]
    +s/no-s confusion; ignorance of true nucleus of noun phrase

VERB/AUX-AGREEMENT WITH TIME [6 and 13:6]
    Lack of agreement with general context, with time signal, with other verbs, in complex sentences, and/or with compound noun clauses

MODIFIERS [8]
    Incorrect form (*-ing/d-t-n*, adjective/adverb, etc.); incorrect order; incorrect position in sentence

COMPARATIVES AND SUPERLATIVES [8:7, 8:8]
    Inappropriate comparison; incorrect comparative formation, inappropriate superlative; incorrect superlative formation

BASIC SENTENCE STRUCTURE [7]
    Incorrect syntax (word order); incorrect shifter; omitted object with transitive verb

EXPLETIVES *there* or *it* (Dummy Subjects) [3:4, 13]
    Unnecessarily used; omitted when needed; followed by incorrect form of verb/aux-word

INCOMPLETE SENTENCES (Fragments) [7, 8, 11, and 12]
    Omission of subject; omission of verb; prepositional phrase used alone; subordinate clause used alone; noun phrase used alone; half-sentence used alone

COORDINATION (Compounding) [10]
    Run-on sentences; comma splice; faulty parallelism; incorrect conjunction choice; incorrect compounding method; unnecessary repetition

SUBORDINATE CLAUSES [11]
    Incorrect clause formation; poor relationship to main sentence; incorrect subordinator

RELATIVE CLAUSES [11]
    Incorrect clause formation; poor relationship to modified noun; incorrect relative pronoun

HALF-SENTENCES (Participial Phrases, Absolute Phrases) [12]
    Incorrect formation; poor relationship to main sentence; different subjects

NOMINAL CLAUSES OR PHRASES [13]
    Incorrect clause formation; incorrect introducer or substitutor; poor relationship; *-ing/to* + base form misuse/confusion

PASSIVE TRANSFORMATION [9:1]
    Used inappropriately; incorrect formation

INDIRECT OBJECT TRANSFORMATION [9:2]
    Used inappropriately; incorrect formation

TRANSITION WORDS [15:1]
    Not used when called for; used inappropriately; poor or incorrect choice

VARIETY IN WRITING [7, 12:7, and 15:2]
    Insufficient variety of basic sentence patterns; insufficient variety of combining methods

COMMAS [7:3, 10, 11, 12, 14]
    Incorrect use with shifters; comma splice; incorrect use with relative clauses; incorrect use with half-sentences; incorrect use with (non-restrictive) added information

VOCABULARY [All Chapters]
    Too limited; incorrect word choice

PREPOSITIONS [*Dyad Learning Program: Prepositions*]
    Incorrect choice; omitted when needed; unnecessarily used

OTHER PROBLEMS

ESSAY #1

English Second Language

Briefly explain how you studied English before you came here. Then, explain how you plan to study English now. Finally, point out some of the differences and similarities between your two methods of studying English.

One of the greatest links that helps to unit [spelling] all the variety [word derivation]

tribes in my country are [verb/aux agreement w/subj. ignorance of true nucleus] the common usage of △ [article omitted] English language.

I began the study of △ [article omitted] English language during my fourth year in

primary school. Among [preposition incorrect] other pupils, I began to learn some

English names for both proper and common nouns.

In 1969, I passed the entrance to Grammar School [capitalization]. I spent

five years in the [article unnecessary] grammar school △ [comma omitted non-restrictive] which [subordinator incorrect] English is the medium

of instructions [noun count/noncount]. In the [article unnecessary] grammar school, my learning of English

advanced much more than the primary school [comparison inappropriate]. It was in [expletive unnecessary]

grammar School [capitalization], I learnt to do comprehension and precis.

My study of △ [article omitted] Latin language for five years helped me a great [modifier]

deal [position] to improve my vocabularies [noun count/noncount].

I arrived at here [preposition unnecessary] to meet △ [article omitted] entirely [spelling] different method of

learning English. It is my candid opinion that the

visual aid [noun s/p] and method of teaching English here is of [verb/aux agreement with subject]

immense assistance to we [pronoun incorrect form] foreign students.

Diagnostic/Referral Checklist

✓	WORD DERIVATIONS (Forms of Content Words) [1] Noun, verb, adjective, and adverb form confusion/misuse
✓✓✓✓✓	ARTICLES [2 and *Dyad Learning Program: Determiners*] Incorrect choice; <u>unnecessarily used</u>; <u>omitted when needed</u>
✓✓✓	NOUNS [2] <u>Singular-plural</u> or <u>count-noncount confusion/misuse</u>; failure to use proper unit expression with noncount noun
✓	PRONOUNS [3 and *Dyad Learning Program: Pronouns*] Lack of agreement with antecedent; ambiguous antecedent; no antecedent; unnecessarily used; not used when called for, <u>incorrect form</u>
	AUXILIARIES AND MODALS (Aux-words) [4] Incorrect choice; omitted when needed; unnecessarily used
	VERB FORMS [5, 7, and *Dyad Learning Program: Verb Forms and Verb Choices*] Incorrect form (base, d-t-n, -ing, +s, no-s, past); incorrect verb choice; unnecessarily used; omitted when needed; incorrect use of two-word verbs
✓✓	VERB/AUX-AGREEMENT WITH SUBJECT (Harmony, Concord) [4, 5, 8:1 and *Dyad Learning Program: Verb Forms*] +s/no-s confusion; <u>ignorance of true nucleus of noun phrase</u>
	VERB/AUX-AGREEMENT WITH TIME [6 and 13:6] Lack of agreement with general context, with time signal, with other verbs, in complex sentences, and/or with compound noun clauses
✓	MODIFIERS [8] Incorrect form (-ing/d-t-n, adjective/adverb, etc.); incorrect order; <u>incorrect position in sentence</u>
✓	COMPARATIVES AND SUPERLATIVES [8:7, 8:8] <u>Inappropriate comparison</u>; incorrect comparative formation, inappropriate superlative; incorrect superlative formation
	BASIC SENTENCE STRUCTURE [7] Incorrect syntax (word order); incorrect shifter; omitted object with transitive verb
✓	EXPLETIVES *there* or *it* (Dummy Subjects) [3:4, 13] <u>Unnecessarily used</u>; omitted when needed; followed by incorrect form of verb/aux-word
	INCOMPLETE SENTENCES (Fragments) [7, 8, 11, and 12] Omission of subject; omission of verb; prepositional phrase used alone; subordinate clause used alone; noun phrase used alone; half-sentence used alone
	COORDINATION (Compounding) [10] Run-on sentences; comma splice; faulty parallelism; incorrect conjunction choice; incorrect compounding method; unnecessary repetition
✓	SUBORDINATE CLAUSES [11] Incorrect clause formation; poor relationship to main sentence; <u>incorrect subordinator</u>
	RELATIVE CLAUSES [11] Incorrect clause formation; poor relationship to modified noun; incorrect relative pronoun
	HALF-SENTENCES (Participial Phrases, Absolute Phrases) [12] Incorrect formation; poor relationship to main sentence; different subjects
	NOMINAL CLAUSES OR PHRASES [13] Incorrect clause formation; incorrect introducer or substitutor; poor relationship; -ing/to + base form misuse/confusion
	PASSIVE TRANSFORMATION [9:1] Used inappropriately; incorrect formation
	INDIRECT OBJECT TRANSFORMATION [9:2] Used inappropriately; incorrect formation
	TRANSITION WORDS [15:1] Not used when called for; used inappropriately; poor or incorrect choice
	VARIETY IN WRITING [7, 12:7, and 15:2] Insufficient variety of basic sentence patterns; insufficient variety of combining methods
✓	COMMAS [7:3, 10, 11, 12, 14] Incorrect use with shifters; comma splice; incorrect use with relative clauses; incorrect use with half-sentences; <u>incorrect use with (non-restrictive) added information</u>
	VOCABULARY [All Chapters] Too limited; incorrect word choice
✓✓	PREPOSITIONS [*Dyad Learning Program: Prepositions*] Incorrect choice; omitted when needed; <u>unnecessarily used</u>
✓✓	OTHER PROBLEMS *Spelling* ✓✓ *Capitalization*

ESSAY #2

English Second Language

Briefly explain how you studied English before you came here. Then, explain how you plan to study English now. Finally, point out some of the differences and similarities between your two methods of studying English.

In my country we △English schools in many places. In
<verb omitted> <preposition incorrect>

one of them I am studying. In the beginning they teach △
<verb agreement with time> <article omitted>

basic of English. In the middle school they start teaching
<noun s/p>

grammer. Every day we have regular English class. Even though
<spelling> <verb-time> <incomplete>

we have our own native language. We △ suppose to speak
<verb-time> <aux omitted> <verb form>
<sentence--subordinate clause used alone>

English, because △ my country we go more language.
<preposition omitted> <vocabulary incorrect word> <vocabulary word> <noun s/p>

There are different ways how I study English before I
<verb-time> <verb-time>
<expletive unnecessarily used and basic sentence structure>

come to here. Actually, I read books in different kind at home.
<verb-time> <preposition unnecessary> <transition word inappropriate> <preposition incorrect> <word order> <noun s/p>

Every Friday night I go and see movies with the subscription
<verb-time> <verb-time> <vocabulary incorrect word>

to improve my reading rate.

These are the differences and similarity of the two methods
<noun s/p>

mention above. First, I did not have a friend who speak
<modifier—incorrect form> <transition word inappropriate> <verb-time>

English as △ first language but now I do have. I did not
<article or possessive omitted> <verb unnecessary—compounding incorrect>

have the proper material but now I do have. Its similarity
<verb unnecessary—compounding incorrect> <pronoun or article>

is that every class discussion was conducted in English

and now at this University every thing is conducted in English.
<compounding incorrect—unnecessary repetition>

Coming to a country having native language English, I hope
<clause formation incorrect>

I can learn English more easily. I enjoy learn new language.
<nominal phrase—-ing/base form of verb>

Diagnostic/Referral Checklist

	WORD DERIVATIONS (Forms of Content Words) [1]
	Noun, verb, adjective, and adverb form confusion/misuse
✓✓✓	ARTICLES [2 and *Dyad Learning Program: Determiners*]
	Incorrect choice; unnecessarily used; <u>omitted when needed</u>
✓✓✓✓	NOUNS [2]
	<u>Singular-plural</u> or count-noncount confusion/misuse; failure to use proper unit expression with noncount noun
✓	PRONOUNS [3 and *Dyad Learning Program: Pronouns*]
	Lack of agreement with antecedent; <u>ambiguous antecedent</u>; no antecedent; unnecessarily used; not used when called for; incorrect form
✓	AUXILIARIES AND MODALS (Aux-words) [4]
	Incorrect choice; <u>omitted when needed</u>; unnecessarily used
✓✓	VERB FORMS [5, 7, and *Dyad Learning Program: Verb Forms and Verb Choices*]
	<u>Incorrect form</u>(base, *d-t-n*, *-ing*, *+s*, *no-s*, past); incorrect verb choice; unnecessarily used; omitted when needed; incorrect use of two-word verbs
	VERB/AUX-AGREEMENT WITH SUBJECT (Harmony, Concord) [4, 5, 8:1 and *Dyad Learning Program: Verb Forms*]
	+s/no-s confusion; ignorance of true nucleus of noun phrase
✓✓✓✓✓✓✓	VERB/AUX-AGREEMENT WITH TIME [6 and 13:6]
	<u>Lack of agreement with general context</u>, with time signal, with other verbs, in complex sentences, and/or with compound noun clauses
✓	MODIFIERS [8]
	<u>Incorrect form</u> (*-ing/d-t-n*, adjective/adverb, etc.); incorrect order; incorrect position in sentence
	COMPARATIVES AND SUPERLATIVES [8:7, 8:8]
	Inappropriate comparison; incorrect comparative formation; inappropriate superlative; incorrect superlative formation
✓✓	BASIC SENTENCE STRUCTURE [7]
	<u>Incorrect syntax (word order)</u>; incorrect shifter; omitted object with transitive verb
✓	EXPLETIVES *there* or *it* (Dummy Subjects) [3:4, 13]
	<u>Unnecessarily used</u>; omitted when needed; followed by incorrect form of verb/aux-word
✓	INCOMPLETE SENTENCES (Fragments) [7, 8, 11, and 12]
	Omission of subject; omission of verb; prepositional phrase used alone; <u>subordinate clause used alone</u>; noun phrase used alone; half-sentence used alone
✓✓✓	COORDINATION (Compounding) [10]
	Run-on sentences; comma splice; faulty parallelism; incorrect conjunction choice; <u>incorrect compounding method</u>; unnecessary repetition
	SUBORDINATE CLAUSES [11]
	<u>Incorrect clause formation</u>; poor relationship to main sentence; incorrect subordinator
✓	RELATIVE CLAUSES [11]
	<u>Incorrect clause formation</u>; poor relationship to modified noun; incorrect relative pronoun
	HALF-SENTENCES (Participial Phrases, Absolute Phrases) [12]
	Incorrect formation; poor relationship to main sentence; different subjects
✓	NOMINAL CLAUSES OR PHRASES [13]
	Incorrect clause formation; incorrect introducer or substitutor; poor relationship; <u>-ing/to</u> + <u>base form misuse/confusion</u>
	PASSIVE TRANSFORMATION [9:1]
	Used inappropriately; incorrect formation
	INDIRECT OBJECT TRANSFORMATION [9:2]
	Used inappropriately; incorrect formation
✓✓	TRANSITION WORDS [15:1]
	Not used when called for; <u>used inappropriately</u>; poor or incorrect choice
	VARIETY IN WRITING [7, 12:7, and 15:2]
	Insufficient variety of basic sentence patterns; insufficient variety of combining methods
	COMMAS [7:3, 10, 11, 12, 14]
	Incorrect use with shifters; comma splice; incorrect use with relative clauses; incorrect use with half-sentences; incorrect use with (non-restrictive) added information
✓✓	VOCABULARY [All Chapters]
	Too limited; <u>incorrect word choice</u>
✓✓✓	PREPOSITIONS [*Dyad Learning Program: Prepositions*]
	<u>Incorrect choice</u>; <u>omitted when needed</u>; <u>unnecessarily used</u>
✓	OTHER PROBLEMS *Spelling*

ESSAY #3

Native Speaker (non-standard dialect)

Why are you at the university? Exactly what do you hope to accomplish while you are here, and how do you plan to accomplish it?

I come to college because I knew it △ be a
                                      aux omitted
great experience. I wanted to meet people from other
place. to see what their life were compare to mine.
noun s/p   noun s/p   modifier—incorrect form

I wanted to learn some of their traditions, beliefs, etc.

I just like meet people and make friend with people from
         nominal phrase—ing/to+base form of verb   noun s/p

all over. I planned △ do this by just mingling with them
                    "to" omitted

on and off campus. Also by participating in as many
                                              incomplete sentence—

extra curricular activities as I can with them. I came here
         half-sentence used alone

because I knew that it was a good school academic. The
                                            word derivation or
                                            modifier position

teachers here are of the finest quality and Compares with any
                                             verb agreement w/subject

other faculties in the nation. Another reason I came here
       noun count/noncount

is because I plan to move here after I finish college.

Attending school at the University and environment around here, it
         half-sentence—different subjects   article omitted   pronoun
                                                                     agreement

help familarize me more with the area. In my first couple △
verb agreement   preposition
with subject   omitted

years at the University I hope to establish a major in

business or physical education or elementary education. By taking
                    compounding incorrect   preposition
                                                             unnecessary

certain classes in these areas and also fulfill my own personal
compounding incorrect— faulty parallelism

goals should help me to choose a definite major.

Diagnostic/Referral Checklist

✓   **WORD DERIVATIONS** (Forms of Content Words) [1]
     Noun, verb, adjective, and <u>adverb</u> form confusion/misuse

✓   **ARTICLES** [2 and *Dyad Learning Program: Determiners*]
     Incorrect choice; unnecessarily used; <u>omitted when needed</u>

✓✓✓✓   **NOUNS** [2]
     <u>Singular-plural</u> or count-noncount confusion/misuse; failure to use proper unit expression with noncount noun

✓   **PRONOUNS** [3 and *Dyad Learning Program: Pronouns*]
     <u>Lack of agreement with antecedent;</u> ambiguous antecedent; no antecedent; unnecessarily used; not used when called for; incorrect form

✓   **AUXILIARIES AND MODALS** (Aux-words) [4]
     Incorrect choice; <u>omitted when needed;</u> unnecessarily used

VERB FORMS [5, 7, and *Dyad Learning Program: Verb Forms and Verb Choices*]
     Incorrect form (base, *d-t-n*, *-ing*, *+s*, *no-s*, past); incorrect verb choice; unnecessarily used; omitted when needed; incorrect use of two-word verbs

✓✓   **VERB/AUX-AGREEMENT WITH SUBJECT** (Harmony, Concord) [4, 5, 8:1 and *Dyad Learning Program: Verb Forms*]
     +s/no-s confusion; <u>ignorance of true nucleus of noun phrase</u>

VERB/AUX-AGREEMENT WITH TIME [6 and 13:6]
     Lack of agreement with general context, with time signal, with other verbs, in complex sentences, and/or with compound noun clauses

✓✓   **MODIFIERS** [8]
     Incorrect form (*-ing/d-t-n*, adjective/adverb, etc.); incorrect order; <u>incorrect position in sentence</u>

COMPARATIVES AND SUPERLATIVES [8:7, 8:8]
     Inappropriate comparison; incorrect comparative formation, inappropriate superlative; incorrect superlative formation

BASIC SENTENCE STRUCTURE [7]
     Incorrect syntax (word order); incorrect shifter; omitted object with transitive verb

EXPLETIVES *there* or *it* (Dummy Subjects) [3:4, 13]
     Unnecessarily used; omitted when needed; followed by incorrect form of verb/aux-word

✓   **INCOMPLETE SENTENCES** (Fragments) [7, 8, 11, and 12]
     Omission of subject; omission of verb; prepositional phrase used alone; subordinate clause used alone; noun phrase used alone; <u>half-sentence used alone</u>

COORDINATION (Compounding) [10]
     Run-on sentences; comma splice; <u>faulty parallelism,</u> incorrect conjunction choice; incorrect compounding method; unnecessary repetition

SUBORDINATE CLAUSES [11]
     Incorrect clause formation; poor relationship to main sentence; incorrect subordinator

RELATIVE CLAUSES [11]
     Incorrect clause formation; poor relationship to modified noun; incorrect relative pronoun

✓   **HALF-SENTENCES** (Participial Phrases, Absolute Phrases) [12]
     Incorrect formation; poor relationship to main sentence; <u>different subjects</u>

✓   **NOMINAL CLAUSES OR PHRASES** [13]
     Incorrect clause formation; incorrect introducer or substitutor; poor relationship; <u>*-ing/to* + base form misuse/confusion</u>

PASSIVE TRANSFORMATION [9:1]
     Used inappropriately; incorrect formation

INDIRECT OBJECT TRANSFORMATION [9:2]
     Used inappropriately; incorrect formation

TRANSITION WORDS [15:1]
     Not used when called for; used inappropriately; poor or incorrect choice

VARIETY IN WRITING [7, 12:7, and 15:2]
     Insufficient variety of basic sentence patterns; insufficient variety of combining methods

COMMAS [7:3, 10, 11, 12, 14]
     Incorrect use with shifters; comma splice; incorrect use with relative clauses; incorrect use with half-sentences; incorrect use with (non-restrictive) added information

VOCABULARY [All Chapters]
     Too limited; incorrect word choice

✓✓   **PREPOSITIONS** [*Dyad Learning Program: Prepositions*]
     Incorrect choice; <u>omitted when needed;</u> <u>unnecessarily used</u>

OTHER PROBLEMS

ESSAY #4

Native Speaker (non-standard dialect)

Why are you at the university? Exactly what do you hope to accomplish while you are here, and how do you plan to accomplish it?

I have always wanted to attended [verb form incorrect] a college. I have planned to attend for quite some time. In preparing and making my future a more pleasant and successful one. [incomplete sentence — half-sentence used alone] I hope to be able to receive [basic sentence structure object omitted] in earning a degree in the field of office management. I hope that I will be able to learn the different type [noun/s/p] of cultural [word derivation] and the ways of life that is set for them. [verb/aux agreement with subject] I hope that by attending college [preposition incorrect] that [nominal clause formation incorrect—introducer repeated] people will accept me and help [vocabulary—incorrect word] the fact that, [comma unnecessary] we as student [noun s/p] have something in common. I hope also to be able to learn alot [spelling] more interesting things [comparison incorrect] in the various clubs and in [preposition incorrect] getting involve [modifier—incorrect form] in all sorts of activities the university has to offered [verb form incorrect] us. And finally, [comma omitted] having these [pronoun—ambiguous antecedent] all adds up to improving myself as a person in trying to prepare [preposition and article omitted] future. Having to set goals, it makes me [half sentence—different subjects] realize how wonderful it is to be a student and going [compounding—faulty parallelism] to a school that can really help me alot. [spelling] The accomplishment [vocabulary—incorrect word] that I have is to strive for the best. In seeking and choosing the right decision for myself and my family. [incomplete sentence—half-sentence used alone]

Diagnostic/Referral Checklist

_____ ✓   **WORD DERIVATIONS** (Forms of Content Words) [1]
Noun, verb, adjective, and adverb form confusion/misuse

_____ ✓   **ARTICLES** [2 and *Dyad Learning Program: Determiners*]
Incorrect choice; unnecessarily used; omitted when needed

_____ ✓✓   **NOUNS** [2]
Singular-plural or count-noncount confusion/misuse; failure to use proper unit expression with noncount noun

_____ ✓   **PRONOUNS** [3 and *Dyad Learning Program: Pronouns*]
Lack of agreement with antecedent; ambiguous antecedent; no antecedent; unnecessarily used; not used when called for; incorrect form

_____   **AUXILIARIES AND MODALS** (Aux-words) [4]
Incorrect choice; omitted when needed; unnecessarily used

_____ ✓✓   **VERB FORMS** [5, 7, and *Dyad Learning Program: Verb Forms and Verb Choices*]
Incorrect form (base, *d-t-n, -ing,* +*s,* no-*s,* past); incorrect verb choice; unnecessarily used; omitted when needed; incorrect use of two-word verbs

_____ ✓   **VERB/AUX-AGREEMENT WITH SUBJECT** (Harmony, Concord) [4, 5, 8:1 and *Dyad Learning Program: Verb Forms*]
+*s*/no-*s* confusion; ignorance of true nucleus of noun phrase

_____   **VERB/AUX-AGREEMENT WITH TIME** [6 and 13:6]
Lack of agreement with general context, with time signal, with other verbs, in complex sentences, and/or with compound noun clauses

_____ ✓   **MODIFIERS** [8]
Incorrect form (*-ing/d-t-n,* adjective/adverb, etc.); incorrect order; incorrect position in sentence

_____ ✓   **COMPARATIVES AND SUPERLATIVES** [8:7, 8:8]
Inappropriate comparison; incorrect comparative formation, inappropriate superlative; incorrect superlative formation

_____ ✓   **BASIC SENTENCE STRUCTURE** [7]
Incorrect syntax (word order); incorrect shifter; omitted object with transitive verb

_____   **EXPLETIVES** *there* or *it* (Dummy Subjects) [3:4, 13]
Unnecessarily used; omitted when needed; followed by incorrect form of verb/aux-word

_____ ✓✓   **INCOMPLETE SENTENCES** (Fragments) [7, 8, 11, and 12]
Omission of subject; omission of verb; prepositional phrase used alone; subordinate clause used alone; noun phrase used alone; half-sentence used alone

_____ ✓   **COORDINATION** (Compounding) [10]
Run-on sentences; comma splice; faulty parallelism, incorrect conjunction choice; incorrect compounding method; unnecessary repetition

_____   **SUBORDINATE CLAUSES** [11]
Incorrect clause formation; poor relationship to main sentence; incorrect subordinator

_____   **RELATIVE CLAUSES** [11]
Incorrect clause formation; poor relationship to modified noun; incorrect relative pronoun

_____ ✓   **HALF-SENTENCES** (Participial Phrases, Absolute Phrases) [12]
Incorrect formation; poor relationship to main sentence; different subjects

_____ ✓   **NOMINAL CLAUSES OR PHRASES** [13]
Incorrect clause formation; incorrect introducer or substitutor; poor relationship; *-ing/to* + base form misuse/confusion

_____   **PASSIVE TRANSFORMATION** [9:1]
Used inappropriately; incorrect formation

_____   **INDIRECT OBJECT TRANSFORMATION** [9:2]
Used inappropriately; incorrect formation

_____   **TRANSITION WORDS** [15:1]
Not used when called for; used inappropriately; poor or incorrect choice

_____   **VARIETY IN WRITING** [7, 12:7, and 15:2]
Insufficient variety of basic sentence patterns; insufficient variety of combining methods

_____ ✓✓   **COMMAS** [7:3, 10, 11, 12, 14]
Incorrect use with shifters; comma splice; incorrect use with relative clauses; incorrect use with half-sentences; incorrect use with (non-restrictive) added information

_____ ✓✓   **VOCABULARY** [All Chapters]
Too limited; incorrect word choice

_____ ✓✓✓   **PREPOSITIONS** [*Dyad Learning Program: Prepositions*]
Incorrect choice; omitted when needed; unnecessarily used

_____ ✓✓   **OTHER PROBLEMS** *Spelling*

SENTENCE COMBINATION
Writing and Combining Standard English Sentences

Book II

9

PASSIVE AND INDIRECT OBJECT TRANSFORMATIONS

1. THE PASSIVE TRANSFORMATION

1.1 Word order (syntax) in sentences is very important, because in English, much meaning comes from word order.

Note the difference in meaning between the two sentences below:

The Eskimo killed the polar bear. The polar bear killed the Eskimo.

The same words are used in each sentence; however, the word order makes a big difference in meaning.

Normal word order (sometimes called an active construction) is used when the subject is important and necessary to the message being communicated.

1.2 The passive transformation is used when

1. the writer wants to emphasize the object of the basic sentence (i.e., the object is more important than the subject),

Example:

The chemicals polluted the river. (active construction)
The river was polluted by the chemicals. (passive transformation)

2. the subject is unimportant or unnecessary to what is being written, or

Example:

The mail was delivered on time. (passive transformation)
The postman delivered the mail on time. (active construction)

3. the subject of the active construction is understood.

Example:

Jane's purse was stolen. (passive transformation)
(Somebody) stole Jane's purse. (active construction)

1.3   Only pattern No. 1 sentences (sentences with objects—explained in Chapter 7) can be transformed from the active to the passive construction.

The passive sentence transformation follows these ten steps:

Example active construction:
>   In 1966, two lions attacked my uncle.

Step 1.

Find the simple, basic sentence. Remove any shifters.
>   Two lions attacked my uncle.

Step 2.

Locate the object of the sentence. (If there is no object you cannot produce a correct passive construction.)
>   Two lions   attacked   *my uncle.*
>   (subject)   (verb)   (object)

Step 3.

Decide if the object should be emphasized more than the subject or if there is any other reason for putting it first in the sentence (variety, parallelism). (If our example sentence is part of a story about *my uncle,* then it will probably be better to use a passive construction and emphasize *him,* and not the lions.)

If there is no reason for using a passive construction then *do not* use it. Too many passive constructions can ruin otherwise good writing. If there is a reason for using a passive construction, then go ahead with the following steps.

Step 4.

Write the *object* of the active construction as the *subject* of the new passive construction. If the object is a pronoun you will have to change it to its subjective form.
>   *My uncle* . . .

Step 5.

If there is an aux-word or aux-words (except *didn't* and *don't*) in the active construction, use the same one(s) in the passive construction. BE CAREFUL! If the aux-word is *has, have, is, am, are, was, were,* or one of the negative forms of these aux-words, you may have to change it so that it will agree with the new subject. If the aux-word is *do, does,* or *did,* it must be removed. The same time is preserved by using the appropriate form of *be* in Step 6. If the aux-word is *don't, doesn't,* or *didn't,* the first part must be removed, but the negative marker *not* remains. Any adverbs remain in the same position. If there is no aux-word, then skip this step.
>   No aux-word in this example sentence

Step 6.

Determine the verb form used in the active construction and write the same form (past or present) of *be* in the new passive sentence. Once again, be careful with agreement. The form of *be* must agree with the new subject (the old object), so you may have to change it from an *s* form to a no-*s* form or vice versa.
>   My uncle *was* (past form of *be* that agrees with the new singular subject) . . .

Step 7.

Next, write the *d-t-n* form of the verb that was used in the active construction.
>   My uncle was *attacked* (*d-t-n* form of *attack*) . . .

Step 8.

Now write the word *by* and then the old (active construction) subject. If the old subject is a pronoun you will have to change it to its objective form.

> My uncle was attacked *by two lions . . .*

Step 9.

Determine if this agent (what you just added in Step 8, the word *by* plus the old subject) is necessary or desirable. If it is, then leave it in. If it isn't, then take it out.

> My uncle was attacked *by two lions.* (IN)
> My uncle was attacked. (OUT)

Step 10.

Any shifters will remain the same. Put them back in the sentence now.

> *In 1966,* my uncle was attacked by two lions.

Here is another example of the passive transformation. (The instructions have been simplified.)

Now try it again.

Example active construction:

> They were observing her through the window.

1. They were observing her. (remove shifter)
2. They were observing *her.* (locate object)
3. Decide if the object should be placed first. (This depends on a number of factors which are not included in these directions.)
4. *She . . .* (New subject, note that the object pronoun *her* has been changed to the subject pronoun *she*)
5. She *was . . .* (aux-word *were* changed to *was* to agree with the new singular subject)
6. She was *being . . .* (-*ing* form of *be* used because *observing* is the -*ing* form)
7. She was being *observed . . .* (*d-t-n* form of active construction verb *observe*)
8. She was being observed *by them.* (new object, note that the subject pronoun *they* has been changed to the object pronoun *them*)
9. She was being observed. (Decide if agent *by them* is important to the meaning of the sentence. In this example it has been left out.)
10. She was being observed *through the window.* (restore shifter)

1.4 An active to passive transformation is *not* possible with all verb meanings. When active-construction sentences containing certain verbs are transformed to the passive, the meaning of the verb changes and/or is unacceptable.

Examples:

> Joyce married Bill last week.
> > (meaning change) Bill was married by Joyce last week.

> The preacher married Joyce and Bill.
> > (no meaning change) Joyce and Bill were married by the preacher.

Note that *married* has two different meanings in the above sentences.

> The shoe fits her foot perfectly.
> > (unacceptable) Her foot is fitted by the shoe perfectly.

> The salesman fit the shoe to her foot.
> > (acceptable) The shoe was fitted to her foot by the salesman.

Note that *fitted* has two different meanings in the above sentences.

1.5 *Do not overuse the passive.* A common mistake is to use too many passive constructions when writing. (Some people think that using passive construction sentences makes their writing sound "literary." This is not true.) It may sometimes be necessary for you to change passive constructions to active constructions.

When a passive construction without an agent (the original subject of the active sentence) is changed to an active construction, the writer must supply the subject (which may have been stated previously or is understood).

Assignment 1:A

Change the following active sentences into passive constructions. With some sentences the passive construction is not possible. Copy all the sentences in paragraph form.

TIDAL ENERGY

1. The ocean creates tremendous unused energy.

2. The pull of the moon's gravity on the earth's water causes tides.

3. The ocean tides could be man's greatest source of power.

4. The contour of the shoreline frequently determines the size of the tides.

5. In some parts of the world, scientists have measured tides as high as forty feet.

6. Oceanographers can accurately predict the height and time of the tides anywhere on earth.

7. Producing energy from ocean tides does not cause pollution problems.

8. So far, man has not harnessed these tides.

9. Modern technicians have met most of man's technological challenges.

10. Man should use the tides' untapped energy source.

Assignment 1:B

Change the following active sentences into passive construction. With some sentences the passive construction is not possible. Copy all the sentences in paragraph form.

CAMOUFLAGE

1. Men and animals have always used camouflage as a protection against their enemies.

2. Man has decorated or painted warships, ammunition dumps, and soldiers' helmets to conceal them from enemy eyes.

3. However, nature has produced the best camouflage in the world.

4. Brilliantly colored tropical fish hide in the brightly colored coral reefs of the ocean.

5. The white arctic wastes hide the polar bear and the snowy owl.

6. The spotted fawn blends into its forest background.

7. Man has adapted many of nature's techniques in his search for camouflage.

8. Men have developed camouflage clothing.

9. Soldiers camouflage their equipment to prevent the enemy from seeing it.

10. At the present time, man's camouflage methods do not equal nature's methods.

Assignment 1:C

Change the following active sentences into passive construction. With some sentences the passive construction is not possible. Copy all the sentences in paragraph form.

HAZARDOUS HABITS

1. Liquor and tobacco bring on much misery and destruction.

2. Drinking drivers cause well over half of the automobile accidents in the United States.

3. Drinking problems ruin many families.

4. A mother's use of liquor and/or tobacco affects unborn children.

5. Millions of Americans use tobacco.

6. Tobacco can cause heart trouble and cancer.

7. Discarded cigarettes cause many destructive fires.

8. Advertisers must print a health hazard warning on all advertising for cigarettes.

9. The advertisers also print this warning on every package of cigarettes.

10. Perhaps someday, people will wake up to the dangers of death and destruction.

Assignment 1.1:A

Find the passive constructions below and change them from the passive to the active construction. In some sentences it may be necessary to supply the subject. Then write all the sentences in paragraph form.

A FOOTBALL GAME

1. Football is played by many young men.

2. The game is begun by a kick off.

3. The ball is run back by a receiver.

4. Sometimes the ball is run all the way back for a touchdown.

5. The fans' approval is roared.

6. The ball is often passed by the quarterback to one of the ends.

7. Frequently the ball is dropped.

8. Pass interference may be called by a referee.

9. Occasionally the quarterback is sacked by the opposing players for a big loss.

10. The fans are let down when their team fails to win.

Assignment 1.1:B

Find the passive constructions below and change them from the passive to the active construction. In some sentences it may be necessary to supply the subject. Then write all the sentences in paragraph form.

A PARTY

1. The party had been planned by the hostess well in advance.

2. Invitations were sent by her several weeks before the party.

3. They were received by the guests a few days after they were sent.

4. The guests' responses were sent immediately.

5. Final preparations for the party were made.

6. On the night of the party, the guests were welcomed at the door by the hostess.

7. The guests who didn't know each other were introduced.

8. Music was played by a band.

9. Refreshments were served.

10. The party was enjoyed by all who were there.

Assignment 1.1:C

Find the passive constructions below and change them from the passive to the active construction. In some sentences it may be necessary to supply the subject. Then write all the sentences in paragraph form.

A GAME-WINNING PLAY

1. The game was being watched by many people.

2. The game was being lost by the home team.

3. The game was being led by the visitors by one point.

4. In the last inning, two batters had been struck out by the visiting team's pitcher.

5. A fast ball was pitched by the pitcher to the third batter.

6. Then, a curve was thrown.

7. The next pitch was hit by the batter.

8. The ball was knocked high and deep into centerfield.

9. The centerfield fence was hit by the ball.

10. It was caught by the centerfielder as it bounced back off the fence.

11. The game was won by that play.

Assignment 1.2:A

In the sentences below there are some active constructions that will be better in the passive. Change them. Then write all the sentences in paragraph form.

AIR MAIL

1. Today, airplanes and helicopters carry mail through the air.

2. They can carry heavy bags and boxes of mail.

3. They have even flown elephants from India to the United States.

4. Years ago, before people invented airplanes, carrier pigeons delivered air mail.

5. These carrier pigeons carried messages strapped to their legs.

6. These messages had to be very light because the birds were very small.

7. People carried the birds in cages to their destination.

8. They strapped a message in a capsule to the pigeon's leg.

9. When the cages were opened, the birds flew back to their homes.

10. There, they delivered the messages.

Assignment 1.2:B

In the sentences below there are some active constructions that will be better in the passive. Change them. Then write all the sentences in paragraph form.

SURVIVAL IN THE DESERT

1. Man needs food and water to survive in the desert.

2. The more important of these is water.

3. A person can find water holes by watching the direction birds fly at dawn and at dusk.

4. People can also find water inside barrel cactus plants.

5. One must squeeze or chew the pulp to get the liquid.

6. People also find water in the roots of desert trees.

7. These roots are close to the surface and spread for twenty or thirty feet.

8. A person can also collect dew from the limbs of dead brush.

9. People do this at daybreak by wiping the limbs with a cloth and wringing it out.

10. A person can collect about a quart of water in an hour in the early morning.

Assignment 1.2:C

In the sentences below there are some active constructions that will be better in the passive. Change them. Then write all the sentences in paragraph form.

SOCCER FEVER

1. Not many years ago, almost no one in the United States played soccer.

2. Few people knew even the basic rules of the top sport in 140 nations.

3. They considered soccer a foreign sport.

4. People in the United States didn't understand other nations' enthusiasm for soccer.

5. Then, in 1974, the New York Cosmos soccer team recruited Pelé, a retired super star from Brazil.

6. The Brazilian master showed his teammates how to really play soccer.

7. His teammates learned their lessons well.

8. The New York Cosmos won the North American Soccer League championship in 1977.

9. North American Soccer League games now draw large crowds.

10. Soccer fever is sweeping the United States.

11. An estimated one million American boys and girls play youth soccer.

12. Perhaps someday a team from the United States will win the prestigious World Cup.

2. THE INDIRECT OBJECT TRANSFORMATION

2.1   The prepositional phrases to + noun phrase or for + noun phrase often follow the object of certain verbs in sentence pattern no. 1. If the noun phrase following the *to* or *for* receives the object, then the indirect object transformation may be used.

Sentences like those below can be transformed using the indirect object transformation.

Examples:
>   I sold my book to your friend.
>   I sold your friend my book. (indirect object transformation)
>
>   The bride threw her bouquet to Susan.
>   The bride threw Susan her bouquet. (indirect object transformation)
>
>   He bought some candy for the children.
>   He bought the children some candy. (indirect object transformation)

2.2   There are four steps in the indirect object transformation:

Step 1.
Make sure the sentence has an object of the verb. (Sentence pattern no. 1)
>   He gave *a new coat of paint* to the house.
>   object of the verb

Step 2.
Make sure that the noun following *to* or *for* receives the object of the verb. (It may not be a noun of place.)
>   He gave a new coat of paint to *the house.*
>   (receives the new coat of paint)

Step 3.
Move the prepositional phrase (to + noun phrase or for + noun phrase) to a new position between the verb and the object of the verb.
>   He gave *to the house* a new coat of paint.
(It is not possible to stop at this stage. This sentence is ungrammatical. You must continue to Step 4.)

Step 4.
Remove the word *to* or *for.*
>   He gave the house a new coat of paint.
>   (indirect object)

Here is another example sentence with **for** + **noun phrase** instead of **to** + **noun** phrase. The process is the same.

Step 1.

> My grandmother made a *sweater* for my brother.
> > (check for an object of the verb)

Step 2.

> My grandmother made a sweater for *my brother.*
> > (my brother received the sweater)

Step 3.

> My grandmother made *for my brother* a sweater.
> > (move to new position)

Step 4.

> My grandmother made my brother a sweater.
> > (remove *for*)

2.3   Only pattern no. 1 sentences with certain verbs can be transformed.

With some transitive verbs the transformation may be done, but it is not necessary. With other transitive verbs the transformation cannot be done.

Sentences containing the following verbs **may** be transformed:

to + noun phrase		for + noun phrase	
advance	pitch	bake	leave
bring	present	boil	light
deny	promise	build	make
drop	read	buy	mix
end	rent	call	order
extend	sell	catch	pack
feed	send	cook	paint
give	serve	cut	peel
grant	ship	dig	pour
hand	show	do	quote
issue	sing	find	reserve
leave	supply	fry	roast
loan	take	get	save
mail	teach	have	sew
offer	tell		
owe	throw		
pass	write		
pay			

Sentences containing the following verbs **can not** be transformed.

address	explain	repeat
announce	introduce	report
answer	mention	return
cash	open	say
change	prescribe	speak
close	pronounce	suggest
describe	prove	

2.4   With a few verbs, if there is a receiver of the verb's action, the receiver (indirect object) must be put before the object of the verb. (It cannot be placed following *to* or *for.*)

Example:

>The book cost me a lot of money.
>unacceptable————▶The book cost a lot of money to me

The following are some of these verbs:

allow	save
ask	trade
charge	wish
cost	

2.5   When the object of the verb in the basic sentence is a **pronoun,** the indirect object transformation should **not** be done.

Example:

>He read the letter to us.
>He read us the letter.
>
>He read it to us.
>unacceptable————▶He read us it.

2.6   Active construction sentences with indirect objects may be transformed into the passive construction in either of two ways:

1.   The **object** of the verb becomes the new subject.

Example:

>My friends gave me a gift.
>A gift was given me by my friends.

2.   The **indirect object** becomes the new subject.

Example:

>My friends gave me a gift.
>I was given a gift by my friends.

Assignment 2:A

Some of the sentences below have to + noun *or* for + noun *phrases which can be transformed into indirect objects. When possible, make the transformation and then rewrite all the sentences in paragraph form.*

BASEBALLS

1. To start the World Series, an invited dignitary throws the first ball to the catcher.

2. The catcher then hands this ball to the special visitor.

3. Many balls are needed for the World Series games.

4. Some balls are ruined by foul tips.

5. Players usually toss these damaged balls to the fans.

6. Batters frequently hit home run balls into the stands.

7. Collectors offer a lot of money for these balls.

8. During the game, the catcher may hand a ball he thinks is bad to the umpire.

9. The umpire continually throws new balls to the pitcher.

10. When a pitcher is relieved, he hands the ball to the team manager.

11. The team manager, in turn, hands the ball to the new pitcher, and the game continues.

Assignment 2:B

Some of the sentences below have to + noun *or* for + noun *phrases which can be transformed into indirect objects. When possible, make the transformation and then rewrite all the sentences in paragraph form.*

TEACHERS AND TESTS

1. Teachers teach lessons to students.

2. Good teachers give all the help they can to their students.

3. They prepare special materials for them to help them learn.

4. After teaching their students, they give tests to them.

5. They don't give tests to punish the students.

6. They give them to evaluate the students' progress.

7. After they have evaluated the students' progress, teachers must give grades to the students.

8. The school sends a grade report to each student.

9. The students are supposed to show it to their parents.

10. In case they don't, the school sends a duplicate of the report to each student's parents also.

Assignment 2:C

Some of the sentences below have to + noun *or* for + noun *phrases which can be transformed into indirect objects. When possible, make the transformation and then rewrite all the sentences in paragraph form.*

HALLOWEEN

1. Halloween is a fun holiday for children.

2. Some parents buy costumes for their children.

3. Other parents make costumes for their children.

4. The children go from door to door in the evening.

5. They say, "Trick or treat," to people in their homes.

6. The people give candy to the children.

7. Some parents have parties for their children.

8. They prepare treats for them.

9. They tell scary stories to them.

10. After Halloween, people begin to prepare for Thanksgiving and Christmas.

Assignment 3.1:A

Write a descriptive paragraph about your **favorite book** *using at least three passive constructions and three indirect object transformations. Underline each of them.*

Assignment 3.1:B

Write a descriptive paragraph about your **favorite food** *using at least three passive constructions and three indirect object transformations. Underline each of them.*

Assignment 3.1:C

Write a descriptive paragraph about your **favorite game** *using at least three passive constructions and three indirect object transformations. Underline each of them.*

10
COMPOUNDING

1. COMPOUNDING SENTENCE PARTS

1.1   Simple, basic sentences that are related may be combined into complex sentences in a number of ways.

The most common way to combine two or more related, basic sentences is by compounding them.

1.2   When two or more sentences have the **same predicate** but **different subjects,** the subjects may be compounded by using the words *and* or *or.* This compounding process results in one sentence.

When *and* is used the resulting compound subject is always **plural** because **all** the subjects are related to the predicate. The time-oriented verb form or aux-word must agree with this plural subject.

Example:

Basic Sentences	Combined
Max works in a mine.	Max and Mike work in a mine.
Mike works in a mine.	

Or indicates a **choice** of subjects. When *or* is used the resulting compound subject is either singular or plural, depending on the subject closest to the verb.

Example:

Bob *or* the girls *are* coming tomorrow.
The girls *or* Bob is coming tomorrow.

When **more than two subjects** are combined by compounding, commas are placed between them. The word *and* or *or* is only placed between the last two in the series.

Examples:

Basic Sentences	Combined
Trees need sunlight.	Trees, flowers, grass, and all other plants need sunlight.
Flowers need sunlight.	
Grass needs sunlight.	
All other plants need sunlight.	

Basic Sentences	Combined
Joe borrowed my car.	Joe, Charlie, or somebody else borrowed my car.
Charlie borrowed my car.	
Somebody else borrowed my car.	

1.3 When two or more sentences have the **same subject** but **different predicates**, the predicates may be compounded by using the words *and, or,* or *but.* This compounding process results in one sentence.

But is used to show a **contrast** between the compounded parts.

Example:

Basic Sentences	Combined
Sharks live in water.	Sharks live in water and breathe with gills.
Sharks breathe with gills.	Sharks live in water but don't have scales.
Sharks do not have scales.	Sharks live in water and breathe with gills but don't have scales.

1.4 When related sentences have other parts which are identical, the identical parts are used only once when the sentences are combined by compounding. The **different** parts must be repeated and connected with *and, or,* or *but.*

Examples:

Compound objects

Joe raises *cows.*	Joe raises *cows and sheep.*
Joe raises *sheep.*	

Compound complements of the same kind (e.g., all adjectives)

Susie is *tall.*	Susie is *tall, thin, and good-looking.*
Susie is *thin.*	
Susie is *good-looking.*	

Compound shifters of the same category (e.g., time shifters. Categories of shifters are discussed in Chapter 7, Section 3.)

In the morning, Joe milks cows.	*In the morning and every night,* Joe milks cows.
Every night, Joe milks cows.	

Verb forms following the same aux-word

Stella is *studying.*	Stella is *studying and learning.*
Stella is *learning.*	
The plant may *grow.*	The plant may *grow or die.*
The plant may *die.*	
Bill has *done the work.*	Bill has *done the work and passed the class.*
Bill has *passed the class.*	

Nouns following the same article

My sister bought a *dress.*	My sister bought a *dress, coat, and hat.*
My sister bought a *coat.*	
My sister bought a *hat.*	
The repairman fixed the *washer today.*	The repairman fixed the *washer and refrigerator today.*
The repairman fixed the *refrigerator today.*	

Adjectives of the same class

Voters elect *city officials.*	Voters elect *city, county, state, and national officials.*
Voters elect *county officials.*	
Voters elect *state officials.*	
Voters elect *national officials.*	

Note that in all the above examples of compounding, the parts that are not repeated (not compounded) are exactly the same.

1.5   Sentence parts that are compounded must belong to the same category or class.

Even though the subjects of these sentences are the same, the complements can **not** be compounded.

Examples:

John's father is *a banker.*   (noun complement)
John's father is *handsome.*   (adjective complement)
John's father is *at home.*   (prepositional phrase complement)

There are two reasons why they cannot be compounded:

1. the complements are not of the same kind (one is a noun, one is an adjective, and one is a prepositional phrase), and

2. there is no meaningful relationship between *banker, handsome,* and *at home.*

Parallel construction (an important feature of correct, grammatical writing) means that compounded parts belong to the same category **and** have a meaningful relationship.

Assignment 1:A

Combine sentences in the passage below by using compound subjects, compound predicates, and other compounds. Then write all the sentences in paragraph form. All of the sentences do not *need to be combined.*

EATING STYLES

1. Some people believe that the way a person eats reveals his personality.
2. Some people eat heartily.
3. They sit down at the table.
4. They gobble up everything within reach.
5. Others eat fastidiously.
6. They sit down at the table.
7. They pick up each piece of food carefully.
8. They examine it for a moment.
9. They finally eat it.
10. A few eaters eat in a mixed-up way.
11. They mix up different kinds of food on their plates.
12. They don't mind eating mixed food.
13. They eat gravy in one bite.
14. They eat peas in one bite.
15. They eat meat in one bite.
16. They eat salad in one bite.
17. The opposite style of eating is to keep everything separate.
18. Some people don't like everything all mixed up.
19. Some people eat in a very organized fashion.
20. They start with their vegetable.
21. They finish it before starting their meat.
22. Others rotate their food.
23. They take one bite of one kind of food.
24. They take a second bite of another kind of food.
25. They take a third bite of a third kind of food.
26. They then start the cycle again.

Assignment 1:B

Combine sentences in the passage below by using compound subjects, compound predicates, and other compounds. Then write all the sentences in paragraph form. All of the sentences do not need to be combined.

A WESTERN

1. Would you like to write a western story?
2. Would you like to write a western novel?
3. It's not difficult.
4. All it takes is time and imagination.
5. First you'll need a pad of paper.
6. First you'll need a pencil.
7. First you'll need a place to write.
8. Next decide on the kind of story.
9. Next decide on its location.
10. Your hero should be poor.
11. Your hero should be honest.
12. Your hero should be suspected by the heroine's father.
13. Your hero should be possibly suspected by the reader.
14. The heroine must be beautiful.
15. The heroine must be secretly in love with the hero.
16. The heroine must be willing to sacrifice herself.
17. The heroine must be willing to sacrifice her happiness to save her father and the ranch.
18. The villain desires the girl.
19. The villain desires the gold mine.
20. The villain desires the ranch.
21. The villain desires to destroy the hero.
22. He is willing to lie.
23. He is willing to cheat.
24. He is willing to kill to get what he wants.
25. At the story's end, right must prevail.
26. At the story's end, the hero must rescue the girl.
27. At the story's end, the hero must win her father's gratitude.

Assignment 1:C

Combine sentences in the passage below by using compound subjects, compound predicates, and other compounds. Then write all the sentences in paragraph form. All of the sentences do not need to be combined.

HOUSES

1. People all over the world build houses.
2. People all over the world like their homes.
3. Houses are built in many shapes.
4. Houses are built in many sizes.
5. Houses are built of grass.
6. Houses are built of palm leaves.
7. Houses are built of wood.
8. Houses are built of steel.
9. Houses are built of stone.
10. Houses are built of adobe.
11. Houses are built of brick.
12. Houses are built of plaster.
13. Houses are built of concrete.
14. Houses are built of other materials.
15. The construction may be simple.
16. The construction may be complex.
17. Construction must be adapted to the climate.
18. Construction must be adapted to the materials available.
19. Construction must be adapted to the skills of the workers.

2.   COMPOUNDING SENTENCES

2.1   Even sentences with no identical parts may be compounded if(and only if) they are related. When sentences are compounded, each sentence has equal weight. One is not more important than another.

The following words may be used to combine sentences by compounding:

and   (shows coordination)
      I work as a carpenter, and my brother assists me.

or   (shows choice)
      He will come to my house, or I will go to his for the holidays.

but   (indicates contrast)
      I plan to major in psychology, but I may change my mind.

yet   (indicates contrast)
      Bananas won't grow in cold places, yet apples need cold weather.

so   (shows purpose or reason)
      The students wanted to pass the course, so they studied hard.

for   (shows cause or reason)
      No one could get into town, for the roads were blocked.

nor   (used only with compounded *negative* sentences. The negative marker in the second sentence is included in the word *nor*. Also the aux-word must be placed in front of the subject as in yes/no questions.)
Matilda can't sing, nor can she play the piano.
Joseph won't go, nor will he support us.

;   (can be used to compound two *closely related* short sentences. A semicolon does not indicate any relationship in addition to the relationship expressed by the meaning of the basic sentences. The semicolon is also used between sets in a series when there are commas in the sets.)
I never loved her; I never will.

When used for compounding, all of the words (*and, or, but, yet, so, for,* and *nor*) are called **coordinating conjunctions.**

Two sentences **cannot** be joined together with **only a comma.** One of the above conjunctions must be used. The result of combining two sentences with only a comma is called a **comma splice,** a common error in written English.

Assignment 2:A

Write the following in paragraph form, combining sentences 2 and 3; 4 and 5; 7 and 8; 9 and 10; and 11 and 12, using appropriate conjunctions.

THE SABER-TOOTH TIGER

1. There are many different kinds of cats.
2. Some of them are tame.
3. Others are very wild.
4. Some wild cats lived in earlier days.
5. They are not found on the earth today.
6. Among these is the saber-tooth tiger.
7. It was about the size of the present-day tiger.
8. Its body was heavier.
9. The saber-tooth tiger had two eight-inch-long upper teeth.
10. Its name came from these teeth.
11. No one in modern times has ever seen this tiger.
12. Men have reconstructed its appearance from bones found in tar pits.

Assignment 2:B

Write the following in paragraph form, combining sentences 2 and 3; 4 and 5; 6, 7, and 8; 9 and 10; and 11 and 12, using appropriate conjunctions.

THE GREAT AUK

1. Some birds are not able to fly through the air.
2. Penguins cannot fly.
3. The bird known as the Great Auk could not rise from the ground.
4. The Great Auk was as large as a goose.
5. Its wings were very small.

6. Great Auks were able to dive into the ocean.
7. They could swim very well.
8. These birds could not fly away.
9. Great Auks lived on small rocky islands in the North Atlantic.
10. Sailors used to kill them by the thousands.
11. These birds had little chance to escape.
12. Killing Great Auks was great sport.
13. The last Great Auk was seen in 1844.

Assignment 2:C

Write the following in paragraph form, combining sentences 1 and 2; 3 and 4; 5 and 6; 7 and 8; and 9 and 10, using appropriate conjunctions.

SOUND

1. Sound must have some material to pass through.
2. It cannot travel through a vacuum.
3. Sound can travel through a variety of materials.
4. It travels at different speeds through different mediums.
5. Sound travels through dry air at about 700 miles an hour.
6. This is about the speed of a bullet fired from a rifle.
7. Sound goes about 2800 miles an hour through water.
8. It moves faster than this through the ground.
9. Sound goes quite rapidly through air.
10. It travels faster through solids and liquids.

Assignment 2.1:A

Select related sentences from those below and combine them by compounding. You may compound whole sentences, subjects, predicates, or other parts of sentences. You may also make some sentences into single-word adjectives. All of the sentences do not need to be combined. Rewrite them in paragraph form.

LIVING THINGS

All living things need food.
All living things need water.
Some places have a mild climate.
Some places have an abundance of food.
Some places have an abundance of water.
Other places have a very harsh climate.
Other places are very dry.
Other places are very hot.
Other places are very cold.
Other places are icy.
People can travel in search of food.
People can travel in search of water.
Animals can travel in search of food.

Animals can travel in search of water.
Insects can travel in search of food.
Insects can travel in search of water.
Plants cannot travel and look for life's necessities.
Some plants manage to live in hot places.
Some plants manage to live in dry places.
Some plants manage to live in cold places.
Some plants manage to live in icy places.
People cannot live very long in deserts without outside aid.
People cannot live very long in arctic wastes without outside aid.

Assignment 2.1:B

Select related sentences from those below and combine them by compounding. You may compound whole sentences, subjects, predicates, or other parts of sentences. You may also make some sentences into single-word adjectives. All of the sentences do not need to be combined. Rewrite them in paragraph form.

ROPE

Rope making was important in ancient times.

Rope making is important today.

At one time rope was only made by hand.

Today rope is made by hand.

Today rope is made by machines.

In Ancient Egypt rope was made from camel hair.

In Ancient Egypt rope was made from twisted grass.

In Ancient Egypt rope was made from thin copper wire.

Today rope is made from plant fibers.

Today rope is made from metal.

Today rope is made from synthetic fibers.

In Ancient Egypt rope was used for tying animals.

In Ancient Egypt rope was used for getting water from deep wells.

In Ancient Egypt rope was used for pulling large stones.

Today rope is used for many of the same purposes.

Today rope is used for many different purposes.

Today rope is used to support bridges.

Today rope is used to tie things.

Today rope is used to tow vehicles.

Today rope is used to lasso animals.

Today rope is used in construction work.

Today rope is used in many other trades.

Rope is used by campers.

Rope is used by mountain climbers.

Assignment 2.1:C

Select related sentences from those below and combine them by compounding. You may compound whole sentences, subjects, predicates, or other parts of sentences. You may also make some sentences into single-word adjectives. All of the sentences do not need to be combined. Rewrite them in paragraph form.

A NEW KNOT

Sailors have invented knots.

Ropemakers have invented knots.

Hobbyists have invented knots.

They have invented over 4,000 separate knots.

New knots are very rare.

The last new knot was invented in 1958.

It was named the Tarbuck knot.

Now, Dr. Edward Hunter has invented a new knot.

Hunter was doodling with some string.

He put two ends opposite each other.

He made a loop in each of them.

Then he pulled them through.

He liked the resulting knot because it was symmetrical.

He liked the resulting knot because it was easy to tie.

Hunter invented the knot over twenty years ago.

He didn't have it appraised until recently.

A knot consultant checked it against examples in seaman's manuals dating back three centuries.

There was nothing like it.

3.   AUX-WORDS AS PREDICATE SUBSTITUTES

3.1   When two sentences with similar predicates are combined, the second predicate may sometimes be shortened. This shortening process uses aux-words to take the place of verbs and other parts of the second predicate.

Examples:

Basic Sentences

John doesn't smoke cigarettes.
I don't smoke cigarettes.

Combined

John doesn't smoke cigarettes, and I don't either.
John doesn't smoke cigarettes, and neither do I.

Basic Sentences

John goes jogging every day.
I go jogging every day.

Combined

John goes jogging every day, and I do too.
John goes jogging every day, and so do I.

When an aux-word is used in the predicate, the same aux-word is repeated and the rest of the predicate is deleted.

When a time-oriented verb is used, the hidden aux-word must be used and the rest of the predicate is deleted.

3.2   There are two different ways that the aux-words are used.

In one, the aux-word follows the subject.

In the other, the natural order is reversed and the aux-word comes before the subject.

The method depends on the conjunctions that are used.

Method A.

With the following conjunctions, the normal word order is used:

and . . . too	both affirmative sentences
or	both affirmative sentences
either . . . or	both affirmative sentences
and . . . either	both negative sentences
but	one affirmative and one negative sentence
yet	one affirmative and one negative sentence
so (showing cause)	any of the above three combinations

Examples:

He works hard, and I do too.
He doesn't work hard, and I don't either.
He doesn't work hard, but I do.
He words hard, yet I don't.
He works hard, so I do too.
He doesn't work hard, so I don't (either).
He doesn't work hard, so I do.
He works hard, so I don't.

Method B.

With the following conjunctions, the aux-word comes before the subject:

and so	both affirmative sentences
and neither	both negative sentences
nor	both negative sentences

Examples:

He works hard and so do I.
He doesn't work hard and neither do I.
He doesn't work hard, nor do I.

Reverse order is not used when one sentence is affirmative and the other is negative.

Note that the negative in the last two example sentences is carried in *neither* or *nor*; therefore only an affirmative aux-word is used in the second part of the sentence.

Assignment 3:A

Combine the following sentences using both methods. Label your combined sentences A or B, depending on the method used. If one method is not possible, write not possible *after the letter. The first one has been done for you.*

ANIMAL EYES

1. Some animals have a complex eye structure.
    Other animals do not have a complex eye structure.
    A. Some animals have a complex eye structure, but other animals don't.
    B. Not possible.

2. The night-crawling earthworm is eyeless.
    Most other animals aren't eyeless.

3. Some animals can't see well in the dark.
    Other animals can see well in the dark.

4. Night hunting owls have enormous eyes.
    The tarsier, a cousin of the monkey, has enormous eyes.

5. A flying squirrel has large eyes also.
    The mole rat doesn't have large eyes.

6. Chameleons have independent swivel eyes.
   Most animals don't have independent swivel eyes.

7. Many animals' eyes can't reflect light.
   A cat's eyes can reflect light.

8. A hawk's eyes outweigh its brain.
   An eagle's eyes outweigh its brain.

9. Moles live in almost complete darkness.
   Shrews live in almost complete darkness.

10. Most mollusks don't have two rows of eyes.
    A scallop has two rows of eyes.

11. Some animals have compound eyes.
    Others don't have compound eyes.

12. Cats can see well in both the light and the dark.
    Geckos can see well in both the light and the dark.

13. Most fish don't have eyes that can see up and down at the same time.
    One special tropical fish has eyes that can see up and down at the same time.

Assignment 3:B

Combine the following sentences using both methods. Label your combined sentences A or B, depending on the method used. If one method is not possible, write not possible *after the letter.*

FISH BAIT

1. Salt water fishermen use bait.
   Fresh water fishermen use bait.

2. Some fishermen use live bait when fishing.
    Other fishermen don't use live bait when fishing.

3. Live bait consists of insects, worms, and fish.
    Plastic bait consists of insects, worms, and fish.

4. Fresh bait isn't expensive.
    Plastic bait is expensive.

5. Plastic lures are used by some fishermen.
    Plastic lures are not used by others.

6. Fresh bait doesn't last for more than one good strike.
    Plastic bait lasts for more than one good strike.

7. Live bait moves by itself.
    Plastic bait doesn't move by itself.

8. Using live bait doesn't require lots of practice.
    Using plastic bait requires lots of practice.

9. A plastic lure has to be moved very slowly.
    Live bait doesn't have to be moved very slowly.

10. Plastic bait must be jerked at just the right time to catch large game fish.
    Live bait must be jerked at just the right time to catch a large game fish.

11. Some fishermen have changed to using plastic lures.
    Others have not changed to using plastic lures.

Assignment 3:C

Combine the following sentences using both methods. Label your combined sentences A or B, depending on the method used. If one method is not possible, write not possible *after the letter.*

THE ARMADILLO

1. The armadillo has traveled a great distance from its traditional home in South America.
   Other wild animals have traveled a great distance from their traditional homes in South America.

2. Most of these wild animals are struggling for survival.
   The armadillo isn't struggling for survival.

3. This wild animal is flourishing throughout the United States.
   Other wild animals aren't flourishing throughout the United States.

4. Most wild animals don't like cleared land.
   The armadillo likes cleared land.

5. The armadillo likes fruit and vegetables.
   Some other wild animals don't like fruits and vegetables.

6. Most animals have some sort of defense mechanism.
   The armadillo has some sort of defense mechanism.

7. The armadillo has sharp claws.
   Some other animals have sharp claws.

8. A frightened armadillo can bury itself in hard dirt in about a minute.
   Most other animals can't bury themselves in hard dirt in about a minute.

9. The armadillo has a very hard skin.
   Some other animals have very hard skins.

10.   An armadillo can curl itself into a ball, completely covered by its hard skin.
       Most other animals with hard skins can't curl themselves into a ball, completely covered by their hard skins.

11.   Some wild animals can't live in ice and snow.
       The armadillo can't live in ice and snow.

12.   The cold areas of the United States are safe from the pesky armadillo.
       Other areas of the United States aren't safe from the pesky armadillo.

Assignment 3.1:A

Select related sentences from those below and combine them. (All of the sentences do not need to be combined.) Then rewrite the entire passage in paragraph form.

CARVING

Carving is an ancient art.
Some carved items are both useful and ornamental.
Wood is a popular material for carving.
Most countries have distinctive styles of carving.
Popular carved items are trays.
Some carved items are useful.
Popular carved items are plates.
Some people collect carvings of animals.
Most ethnic groups have distinctive styles of carving.
Others collect different kinds of carvings.
Some carved items are very large.
Popular carved items are bowls.
Carving is still popular today.
Popular carved items are mugs.
Others are ornamental.
Ivory is a popular material for carving.
Others are very small.

Assignment 3.1:B

Select related sentences from those below and combine them. (All of the sentences do not need to be combined.) Then rewrite the entire passage in paragraph form.

PIGS: INTELLIGENCE AND COURAGE

People have enjoyed eating pigs for many centuries.

Pigs are intelligent animals.

A pig's sense of smell is keener than a dog's.

One brave mother pig fought off a full grown bear.

People have not appreciated pigs' other qualities.

Cats are smart animals.

One sow in England learned to be a good "bird dog."

You can't fool a pig with an empty bucket.

Pigs are courageous.

Horses are smart animals.

Pigs are trained to find truffles growing deep underground by smelling them.

Pigs make decisions by balancing pleasure against pain.

One sow in England watched hunting dogs perform.

Dogs are smart animals.

This pig kept investigating police at bay for nearly an hour.

Pigs arrive at solutions to problems by thinking them through.

One brave mother pig protected her young piglets.

You can fool a horse with an empty bucket.

One pig was trained to guard a garden plot growing marijuana.

Pigs are the smartest animals in the barnyard.

Pigs are smarter than all three of these animals.

Assignment 3.1:C

Select related sentences from those below and combine them. (All of the sentences do not need to be combined.) Then rewrite the entire passage in paragraph form.

PIGS: MEAT AND MEDICINE

Pigs, like poets, are never appreciated until they are dead.

Adult hogs usually weigh about 800 pounds.

In recent years, scientists have bred special mini-pigs.

Pigs are not liked for their intelligence.

Pigs come in all sizes.

These chemical derivatives extend human life.

Pig skin sticks without an adhesive.

Pigs are liked for the meat they produce.

The heaviest pig on record weighed 1,904 pounds.

These chemical derivatives alleviate suffering.

Pig skin is easy to remove from the burn.

Modern pigs require less than six pounds of feed to produce one pound of pork.

Pigs are not liked for their courage.

Physiologically, pigs are very similar to men.

Pig skin is an excellent bandage for severe burns.

In the past dozen years, pork has increased in protein by one-fifth.

These mini-pigs are used as replacements for humans in laboratory research.

Hundreds of chemical derivatives come from pigs.

Cattle require sixteen pounds of food to produce one pound of beef.

These mini-pigs weigh only 180 pounds as adults.

Valves from pig hearts are used to replace defective valves in human hearts.

These chemical derivatives are used for medical purposes.

Over 60,000 people are alive today because of a piece of pig in their hearts.

Of all meats, pork is richest in thiamin and iron.

Assignment 3.2A

Write at least twenty basic sentences on the topic **books.** *On another sheet of paper combine the related sentences using the methods shown in this chapter.*

Assignment 3.2:B

Write at least twenty basic sentences on the topic **money.** *On another sheet of paper combine the related sentences using the methods shown in this chapter.*

Assignment 3.2:C

Write at least twenty basic sentences on the topic **exercise.** *On another sheet of paper combine the related sentences using the methods shown in this chapter.*

11
SUBORDINATE
AND RELATIVE CLAUSES

1. SUBORDINATE CLAUSES

1.1 Another method of combining two or more related sentences is to make a subordinate clause of one or more of them and attach it to the front or end of the main sentence.

To make a subordinate clause from a sentence, a word called a **subordinator** is placed at the beginning of the basic sentence.

Here are some common subordinators categorized by meaning:

time		cause or reason	condition	contrast
after	once	as	else	although
as	the next time	as long as	if	even though
as long as	until (till)	because	in case	though
before	when	now (that)	that	
next time	whenever	since	unless	
now	while	so (that)	whatever	
			where	
			whether	

The choice of a subordinator is determined by the relationship between the sentences to be combined.

When a subordinator is added to a sentence, this sentence becomes a **subordinate clause**. It is no longer a sentence and cannot be used alone. If it is used (incorrectly) by itself, it is called a **sentence fragment**.

Only one of the two methods—compounding (Chapter 10) or subordinating—can be used when combining two sentences.

Example:

John loved Grace. John married Susan.

correct———→Although John loved Grace, he married Susan. (subordination)
      John loved Grace, but he married Susan. (compounding)

incorrect———→Although John loved Grace, but he married Susan.

1.2   When subordinators are used, the sentences do not have equal weight as they do in compounds. Shifters have less weight than the main sentence. Except when the relationship between sentences is cause or reason, if one sentence is more important than the other(s), it should be the main sentence. Make the less important sentence a shifter by putting a subordinator in front of it.

Example:

> John loved Grace. John married Susan.
>
> Although John loved Grace, he married Susan.
> > (The girl he married is given more importance.)
>
> Although John married Susan, he loved Grace.
> > (The girl he loved is given more importance.)

When the relationship between two sentences is cause or reason, the sentence which shows cause or reason becomes the subordinate clause.

Examples:

> The dog looked fierce. (cause)
> The boy was afraid. (effect)
>
> Because the dog looked fierce, the boy was afraid.

1.3   Subordinate clauses may be used in either front or end shifter position. When they are used as front shifters, a comma is used to separate them from the main sentence. No comma is used when they follow the main sentence.

Examples:

> The boy was afraid because the dog looked fierce.
> Because the dog looked fierce, the boy was afraid.

Assignment 1:A

Find the subordinate clauses in the following passage. Copy them and label each one time, cause, reason, condition, *or* contrast, *depending on its relationship to the main sentence. The first one has been done for you.*

COOKBOOK RECIPES

If you want to be a good cook you will need a top quality cookbook. Whatever culinary talent you might
condition
have, the ability to follow a recipe is of great importance. Don't be embarrassed because you have to depend on cooking instructions. Even the best cooks depend on the recipes of others when they are learning to prepare a new dish.

> After you become familiar with a recipe you can experiment and modify it. If your experiment suceeds, you can make a note and change the recipe for use on future occasions. If your experiment fails, be sure to note what made it fail. You will not make the same mistake twice unless you forget to make a note of it.

1.   *If you want to be a good cook (condition)*

Assignment 1:B

Find the subordinate clauses in the following passage. Copy them and label each one time, cause, reason, condition, *or* contrast, *depending on its relationship to the main sentence.*

SUPERSTITIONS

Although many people say they don't believe in them, superstititions are very much a part of our lives. Even though they won't admit it, many educated people still perform superstitious actions. If they spill some salt, they are quick to throw a pinch of it over their left shoulder. They may do this simply out of habit or because they really believe that it will keep bad luck and the devil away. When they hear someone sneeze, many modern people say, "Bless you." This centuries-old practice developed because people believed that when a person sneezed his soul left his body. Unless they know they are being watched, many members of our "scientific" society will go out of their way to avoid walking under a ladder. The next time you take a test, look around the room. You may notice several classmates carrying good luck charms, even though they will never admit that they *really* believe in them.

Assignment 1:C

Find the subordinate clauses in the following passage. Copy them and label each one time, cause, reason, condition, *or* contrast, *depending on its relationship to the main sentence.*

COMIC BOOKS

Because they are cheap and because they are easy to read, comic books are very popular. Even though comic books have little educational or literary value, people buy them because they are entertaining. If a person cannot read well, he can still enjoy a comic book. The pictures will tell him what is happening when he can't understand the written words. Young children are the greatest fans of comic books, since the simple yet action-packed plots of the stories the books contain appeal to uneducated intellects. The low prices of comic books also match the limited budgets of most school children. Although they can't afford hardcover books, young people usually have enough money to buy inexpensive comic books. Other children are even more careful with expenses and trade their old comic books with friends whenever they can.

Some adult comic book fans keep "classic" issues and collect them until they have outstanding collections. Although the comic books cost little originally, as "classics" they are worth a great deal.

Assignment 1.1:A

Combine the sentences in each of the groups below by using subordinators. Make sure that you understand the relationship between sentences so that you can select an appropriate subordinator.

TELEVISION PROGRAMS

1. Television programs change frequently in the United States.
    The tastes of TV viewers change constantly.

2. The major TV networks spend millions of dollars to find out what the viewing public wants to see.
    The competition between networks is keen.

3. A sensitive rating system is used to determine program popularity.
    Ratings change nearly every week.

4. A program is popular.
    TV stations charge a lot of money for a few seconds of advertising time.

5. A particular program increases in popularity.
    The price of advertising during that program goes up.

6. The cost of advertising is lower.
    Less popular programs are broadcast.

7. Program times are shuffled.
    TV stations want to broadcast the most popular programs at the best viewing times.

8. A program may be very educational or beneficial in some other way.
    Its popularity with the viewing public is the only thing that is evaluated.

Assignment 1.1:B

Combine the sentences in each of the groups below by using subordinators. Make sure that you understand the relationship between sentences so that you can select an appropriate subordinator.

EARTHQUAKES

1. Compression or tension stresses build up on the earth's surface.
    The earth moves and earthquakes occur.

2. There is a sudden release of stress.
    The movement causes vibrations to pass through and around the earth.

3. Wave vibrations travel through the land.
    Uplifts and landslides occur.

4. Buildings and chimneys fall.
    People are killed or hurt.

5. The vibrations pass through the sea.
    Tsunamis or tidal waves occur.

6. Tidal wave warning systems have been in operation.
    Many people have escaped being washed out to sea.

7. No one knows when or where an earthquake will occur.
    Scientists have ideas about where earth stresses are building up.

8. Earthquakes could be predicted.
    Many lives would be saved.

Assignment 1.1:C

Combine the sentences in each of the groups below by using subordinators. Make sure that you understand the relationship between sentences so that you can select an appropriate subordinator.

ARABLE LAND

1. Man cannot live everywhere on earth.
   Twenty percent of the earth's surface is water.

2. People cannot cultivate all the land on the earth.
   Thirty percent of the land area is frozen ice or glaciers.

3. Very little rain falls on some parts of the land.
   Deserts cover much of the land area.

4. Engineers have reclaimed some desert land.
   Much desert land will never be reclaimed.

5. In some areas, once fertile land has become desert.
   These areas are limited.

6. Floods and tides have eroded away much arable land.
   Engineers have reclaimed some of the shallow ocean floors.

7. Men have built reservoirs for water storage.
   Desert land has been cultivated successfully.

8. People can utilize the sea.
   Less land will be needed to raise food.

Assignment 1.2:A

Complete each of the sentences below by adding a main sentence to the subordinate clause given. Read through the clauses first and be sure that all of your sentences are related and make a connected passage.

BEFORE THE TEST

1. After John finished his work,

2. Although he knew he should study,

3. After that was done,

4. Because he wanted to do well,

5. Since he had read the textbook,

6. Unless he did well,

7. Whatever the outcome would be,

8. In case he needed it,

Assignment 1.2:B

Complete each of the sentences below by adding a main sentence to the subordinate clause given. Read through the clauses first and be sure that all of your sentences are related and make a connected passage.

CHRISTMAS HOLIDAYS

1. Before the Christmas holidays began,

2. Wherever anyone looked,

3. Although their funds were limited,

4. If nothing else was available,

5. Because the family enjoyed being together,

6. When all the preparations were finished,

7. Before the presents were opened,

8. While the family members opened their presents,

9. In spite of the noisy shouts of the children,

10. After the Christmas holidays were over,

Assignment 1.2:C

Complete each of the sentences below by adding a main sentence to the subordinate clause given. Read through the clauses first and be sure that all of your sentences are related and make a connected passage.

THE CONCERT

1. Although tickets are expensive,

2. If one appreciates music,

3. When the concert starts,

4. Because everyone enjoys the music,

5. Even though the concert lasts all evening,

6. Before the performance is over,

7. Even if one gets tired,

8. When one invests time and money,

9. After the program has concluded,

10. Any time another concert is announced,

2. RELATIVE CLAUSES

2.1   When two sentences have a common noun, one may be used to modify that noun in the other sentence. The modifying sentence is turned into a relative clause and placed after the noun it modifies. **A relative pronoun** is used in place of the subject or object of the sentence which is changed to a relative clause.

The following function words are used as relative pronouns:

who (for human subjects)
whom (for human objects)
which (for nonhuman subjects and objects)
that (for both human and nonhuman subjects and objects)
where (for place)
when (for time)
whose (for possession)

To combine two sentences in this way, follow the steps below:

Step 1.

Start with two related sentences with a noun in common. (Any of the basic sentence patterns may be used.)
    The man robbed the bank.
    The man was wearing a ski mask.

Step 2.

Decide which sentence will become the modifying clause. (This should be the least important of the two sentences.)
    The man was wearing a ski mask. (main sentence)
    The man robbed the bank. (modifying sentence)

Step 3.

Substitute the appropriate relative pronoun(*who, whom, which, that,* etc.) for the noun the two sentences have in common.
    The man was wearing a ski mask. (main sentence)
    who robbed the bank (relative clause)

Step 4.

Place the modifying clause after the noun it modifies.
    The man who robbed the bank was wearing a ski mask.

Example:
    Step 1.   The man robbed the bank.
            The bank is on Main Street.
    Step 2.   The man robbed the bank. (main sentence)
            The bank is on Main Street. (modifying sentence)
    Step 3.   The man robbed the bank. (main sentence)
            which is on Main Street (relative clause)
    Step 4.   The man robbed the bank which is on Main Street.

2.2   When the noun in common is the object of the modifying sentence, an additional step (3A) must be added.

Step 1.   The police captured the man.
The man wasn't wearing a ski mask.

Step 2.   The police captured the man. (modifying sentence)
The man wasn't wearing a ski mask. (main sentence)

Step 3.   The police captured whom (*whom* is used because the noun it replaces is used as the object in this sentence)
The man wasn't wearing a ski mask. (main sentence)

Step 3A.   Move the relative pronoun (*whom*) to the front of the relative clause.
whom the police captured

Step 4.   The man whom the police captured wasn't wearing a ski mask.

2.3   The relative pronoun *that* is sometimes used in place of any of the other relative pronouns except *whose*.

Examples:

The man *that* robbed the bank was wearing a ski mask.
The man robbed the bank *that* was on Main Street.
The man *that* the police captured wasn't wearing a ski mask.

2.4   If the relative pronoun replaces the **object** of the relative clause, it is possible to leave it out.

Example:

The man the police captured wasn't wearing a ski mask.

The relative pronoun **cannot** be left out if it replaces the subject of the modifying clause.

2.5   When the information provided by the relative clause is needed to identify the noun it modifies, no commas are used to set it off.

Example:

The person who wrote that book certainly had some wild ideas.

Commas are used to set off a relative clause when the noun that the clause modifies has an identity independent of the information provided by the clause.

Example:

George Washington, who was the first President of the United States, is known as the father of his country.

The use or nonuse of commas to set off a relative clause may change the meaning of the sentence.

Examples:

The students who were late missed the exam. (Only the late students missed the exam.)
The students, who were late, missed the exam. (All the students referred to were late and all of them missed the exam.)

Assignment 3:A

Copy the relative and subordinate clauses in the passage below. After each clause write the noun which it modifies.

COLOR

[1]Color is a strange thing. [2]It exists in light which seems colorless to human eyes. [3]It does not exist in soap bubbles, rainbows, or paint, which all appear colored. [4]The colorful world that we see around us is not really many-hued. [5]Objects which seem colored appear a certain shade because their surfaces reflect back part of the light that is hitting them. [6]Thus, an apple looks red because it reflects red light. [7]The apple, which appears red, is not really that color.

[8]An object that appears to be one color one moment and another color a moment later—such as oil on water—does not really change color. [9]Colors play tricks like these because of variation in light sources and reflective surfaces.

Assignment 3:B

Copy the relative and subordinate clauses in the passage below. After each clause write the noun which it modifies.

THE HORSESHOE CRAB

[1]The horseshoe crab, which is also called a king crab, has a body which is shaped like a horseshoe. [2]Scientists who study this creature, which is related to the spider, say it is not a true crab. [3]Its mouth, which has no jaws, is flanked by a pair of pincers that crush worms and other food. [4]It can burrow through sand or mud because of its five pairs of walking legs. [5]Horseshoe crabs, which are found along the Atlantic Coast, look for food along the bottom of the ocean. [6]Although the water is not clear, the crabs seem to see very well. [7]They can pick out things that other animals do not see. [8]Things that are black appear blacker and things that are white appear whiter to the crab. [9]This crab, which lives in shallow water, sometimes grows to be nearly two feet long.

Assignment 3:C

Copy the relative and subordinate clauses in the passage below. After each clause write the noun which it modifies.

BODY LANGUAGE

[1]People who speak different languages realize they have problems communicating. [2]However, gestures, which everyone frequently uses, are often considered to have only one meaning. [3]People who live in Europe and America think that a nod of the head, which is a gesture all people use, must mean a positive yes. [4]Although most people believe a nod means yes, this is not true in all cultures. [5]Some cultures use a nod to signify no. [6]The sign for OK, which is familiar to all people in the United States, is an obscene gesture in some countries that are located south of the border. [7]Anyone who expects to communicate with people who live in other cultures should try to understand both the verbal language, which can usually be learned through textbooks and teachers, and the meaningful gestures that accompany that language and are often overlooked by language learners.

Assignment 2.1:A

Combine each of the following pairs of sentences by making one of them a relative clause which modifies the noun they have in common. Then write the combined sentences in paragraph form.

ENDANGERED SPECIES

1. The great dodo bird once lived in Africa.
    The great dodo bird could not fly.

2. Dodo birds were bigger than turkeys.
    Until the 1600s there were many dodo birds.

3. There were no laws to protect these dodo birds.
    These dodo birds became extinct.

4. The beautiful whooping crane began to die out.
    The beautiful whooping crane is found in America.

5. At one time there were only about fifty whooping cranes.
    The whooping cranes were disappearing.

6. Laws were enacted to ensure their safety.
    Laws protected the whooping crane.

7. Hundreds of thousands of buffalo were killed indiscriminately.
    Hundreds of thousands of buffalo once lived in North America.

8. Hunters killed the buffalo for sport.
    Hunters almost annihilated the animals.

9. The buffalo almost died out.
    The buffalo once roamed the great plains.

10.   The buffalo are protected by law.
      The buffalo are no longer an endangered species.

11.   One hopes that the whooping crane and the buffalo will not be as dead as the dodo.
      The whooping crane and the buffalo were once nearly extinct.

Assignment 2.1:B

Combine each of the following groups of sentences by making one or more of them a relative clause which modifies the noun they have in common. Then write the combined sentences in paragraph form.

TYPEWRITERS I

1.   Typewriters are used extensively today.
     Typewriters are a relatively recent invention.

2.   The first typewriter was invented in 1714 by Henry Mill.
     The first typewriter was not very practical.
     Henry Mill lived in England.

3.   A different typewriter was invented in 1829 by an American.
     A different typewriter was called the "typographer."
     A different typewriter was the first practical typewriter.

4.   In 1833, another typewriter was developed in France.
     Another typewriter featured many improvements.

5. Many of these original typewriters produced embossed writing.
    Many of these original typewriters were intended for use by the blind.

6. In 1867, a typewriter was developed by Philo Remington.
    This typewriter was the first real commercial typewriter.

7. Seven years later, Remington marketed his typewriter.
    His typewriter typed only capital letters.

8. An improved model came out in 1878.
    An improved model had a shift key and could type both upper and lower case letters.

9. The first electric typewriters appeared in 1935.
    The first electric typewriters allowed typists to produce uniformly dark characters with greater speed and less effort.

Assignment 2.1:C

Combine each of the following pairs of sentences by making one of them a relative clause which modifies the noun they have in common. Then write the combined sentences in paragraph form.

TYPEWRITERS II

1. The stock ticker revolutionized the business investment world.
   The stock ticker was a kind of "automatic" typewriter.

2. Modern communications networks depend on the teletype.
   The teletype is another kind of automatic typewriter.

3. The teletype converts electrical impulses into typed news stories.
   The electrical impulses are sent by telephone or telegraph.

4. More recently, improved electric typewriters have been invented.
   The improved electric typewriters' carriages do not move.

5. A small metal ball moves across the page while the paper remains stationary.
   A small metal ball has raised characters.

6. The ball impresses characters on the paper.
   The ball rotates very quickly.

7. Having several different balls is as good as having several different typewriters.
   Different balls are interchangeable.

8. New models of typewriters continue the trend toward convenience in typing.
   New models offer such features as automatic centering and programmable memories.

9. Since the original development of typewriters, many improvements have been made.
   Many improvements make typing easier and faster.

10. The typewriter continues to play an important role in our daily lives.
    The typewriter has been around for less than two centuries.

Assignment 2.2

Write ten sets of two related sentences each on one of the topics for each assignment below. Each set of sentences should have a common noun. Then combine each set of two sentences into one sentence using a relative pronoun to make one of the sentences modify the common noun.

2.2:A   Trees or Plants

2.2:B   Houses or Buildings

2.2:C   Clubs, Unions, or Churches

Assignment 2.3:A

Write at least twenty basic sentences on the topic of **post offices.** *Combine the related sentences using any of the combining methods that have been presented up to this point.*

Assignment 2.3:B

Write at least twenty basic sentences on the topic of **libraries.** *Combine the related sentences using any of the combining methods that have been presented up to this point.*

Assignment 2.3:C

Write at least twenty basic sentences on the topic of **church buildings.** *Combine the related sentences using any of the combining methods that have been presented up to this point.*

12

HALF-SENTENCES

1. SAME SUBJECT AND AUX-WORD *BE*

1.1 Another method of combining related sentences with the same established time is by making one into a half-sentence,* and attaching it to the main sentence.

This method is used to combine sentences which have the same subject.

Examples:

> John was walking to school this morning.
> John noticed the cherry trees were blooming.
>
> The breaking waves were whipped by the wind.
> The breaking waves threw spray high into the air.

1.2 A sentence which contains one of these aux-words (*am, is, are, was, were*) is made into a half-sentence by dividing the sentence between the aux-word and the verb and removing the first part (the subject and the aux-word).

Examples:

> John was walking to school this morning.
> John was / walking to school this morning.
>> Half-sentence: walking to school this morning.
>
> The breaking waves were whipped by the wind.
> The breaking waves were / whipped by the wind.
>> Half-sentence: whipped by the wind.

1.3 A half-sentence is no longer a complete sentence and cannot stand alone. It must be attached to another sentence. This half-sentence is placed either (1) immediately before the subject, or (2) immediately after the subject of the main sentence (unless the subject is the pronoun *it*).

Examples:

> Walking to school this morning, John noticed the cherry trees were blooming.
> John, walking to school this morning, noticed the cherry trees were blooming.
>
> Whipped by the wind, the breaking waves threw spray high into the air.
> The breaking waves, whipped by the wind, threw spray high into the air.

*Robert L. Allen's term.

Notice that the half-sentence relates directly to the subject. For this reason the two sentences which are combined using this method must have the same subject. The sentences below should not be combined because the resulting sentence would be incorrect or misleading.

John was walking to school this morning.
The cherry trees were blooming.

incorrect———→Walking to school this morning, the cherry trees were blooming.
(Cherry trees don't walk to school.)

Assignment 1:A

If possible, combine each of the following groups of two sentences into one sentence each by making a half-sentence of one of the sentences and then attaching it to the other. Then write the sentences in paragraph form.

THE GREAT TRAIN ROBBERY

1. The Great Train Robbery of 1885 was an unprecedented crime.
   The Great Train Robbery of 1885 occurred in Victorian England.

2. It was called the Crime of the Century.
   It involved many people and tremendous planning.

3. Plans for the robbery were well prepared and coordinated.
   Plans for the robbery took over a year to perfect.

4. Gold was stolen from safes on the train.
   The safes contained gold to pay soldiers in the Crimean War.

5. The amount stolen was large but not the largest to date.
   The amount stolen appeared less significant than the crime itself.

6. The railroads were considered the hallmark of progress.
   The railroads represented the material advancement that would eventually lead to the eradication of crime.

7. Crime was compared to the plague.
   Crime would inevitably disappear with changing social conditions.

8. This crime was not linked to social conditions.
   This crime came from another source.

9. People were absolutely astonished to discover that crime could prey on progress.
    People called this robbery the Crime of the Century.

10. The Great Train Robbery is still remembered 125 years after it took place.
    The Great Train Robbery captures the attention and imagination of all who read about it.

Assignment 1:B

If possible, combine each of the following groups of two sentences into one sentence each by making a half-sentence of one of the sentences and then attaching it to the other. Then write the sentences in paragraph form.

THE TAJ MAHAL

1. The Taj Mahal is one of the most beautiful buildings in the world.
    The Taj Mahal immortalizes the love of the emperor Shah Jahan for his favorite wife.

2. It was built for the tomb of Mumtaz Mahal.
    It has become the symbol of the Eastern world.

2. The building is magnificently proportioned.
    The building awes visitors from all over the world.

4. The Taj Mahal must be seen to be appreciated.
    Many visitors come at full moon to see it.

5. It rises from a platform with buildings of red sandstone at each side.
    It is reflected in a long, rectangular pool.

6. Four famous minarets are judged the most graceful towers in the world.
   Four famous minarets surround it.

7. They are crowned with eight-windowed cupolas.
   They taper to a majestic height of 138 feet.

8. The Taj Mahal was begun in 1630 and completed in 1648.
   The Taj Mahal has remained in excellent condition for about 350 years.

9. An enormous room is inside of the Taj.
   An enormous room contains the octagonal burial chamber of Shah Jahan and Mumtaz Mahal.

10. A famous marble screen encircles the coffin.
    A famous marble screen is carved in filigree that can only be compared to lace.

11. Mosaics are set with thirty-five kinds of rare stones.
    Mosaics decorate the burial chamber in an enormous marble room.

Assignment 1:C

If possible, combine each of the following groups of two sentences into one sentence each by making a half-sentence of one of the sentences and then attaching it to the other. Then write the sentences in paragraph form.

CATALOG BUSINESS

1. Mail order catalogs are an important part of American commerce.
   Mail order catalogs do millions of dollars of business every year.

2. Mail order catalogs allow people to shop without leaving their homes.
   Mail order catalogs are published by many large retail businesses.

3. Several companies are well known because of their catalogs.
   Several companies lead all others in catalog sales.

4. Montgomery Ward was started in 1872.
   Montgomery Ward was the first large store to sell a variety of goods by mail.

5. Sears, Roebuck and Company was started a few years later, in 1886.
   Sears, Roebuck and Company began selling mail order watches.

6. Millions of Americans were scattered throughout rural America.
   Millions of Americans lived far from large stores which offered a wide selection of goods.

7. These rural Americans were looking for a convenient way to purchase the things they needed.
   These rural Americans eagerly requested their catalogs.

8. Their desires for material goods were fired by the many illustrations the catalogs contained.
   Their desires for material goods increased as they read the descriptions of each item in the catalogs.

9. Sears was ahead of Montgomery Ward in sales volume by 1900.
   Sears has never been in second place since that time.

10. Sears is now more than ninety years old.
    Sears has expanded its operations to where more is sold in its stores than through its catalogs.

11. Sears is still the biggest publisher in the entire United States.
    Sears publishes well over three hundred million catalogs per year.

12. Sears, Roebuck and Company accounts for a full one percent of the gross national product of the entire country.
    Sears, Roebuck and Company is the largest retail business in the United States.

2.   SAME SUBJECT AND TIME-INCLUDED VERB FORM

2.1   A sentence which contains a **time-included** verb is made into a half-sentence by

1.   dividing the sentence between the subject and verb,
2.   removing the subject, and then
3.   changing the time-included verb form to the timeless *-ing* form.

The half-sentence formed in this way must be added to the main sentence either

1.   immediately before the subject, or
2.   immediately after the subject of the main sentence.

Example:

John walked to school this morning.
John noticed that the cherry trees were blooming.

1.   Walking to school this morning, John noticed the cherry trees were blooming.
2.   John, walking to school this morning, noticed the cherry trees were blooming.

3.   SAME SUBJECT, AUX-WORD, AND TIMELESS VERB FORM

3.1   A sentence containing the aux-words *will, shall, do, does, did, don't, doesn't,* or *didn't* (followed by the timeless base form of a verb) can also be made into a half-sentence. The aux-word is removed and the base form of the verb is changed to the *-ing* form.

Example:

John will study biology next year.
John will dissect a frog.
Studying biology next year, John will dissect a frog.

If the base form *be* follows these aux-words, it also should be removed.

3.2   When one of the aux-words *don't, doesn't* or *didn't* or *do, does,* or *did* plus *not* (*do not, does not,* or *did not*) is used, the aux-word is removed but the negative *not* remains.

Example:

John didn't know the answers to the test.
John failed the test.
John, not knowing the answers, failed the test.

3.3   Sentences containing the aux-words *have, has,* or *had* (followed by the timeless d-t-n form of the verb) can also be made into half-sentences. In these sentences the aux-word (*have, has,* or *had*) is changed to the timeless *-ing* form *having*. The *d-t-n form* of the verb remains.

Example:

John has had many serious problems in his life.
John endures minor discomforts without complaining.
Having had many serious problems in his life, John endures minor discomforts without complaining.

Assignment 3:A

If possible, combine each of the following groups of two sentences into one sentence each by making a half-sentence of one of the sentences and then attaching it to the other. Then write the combined sentences in paragraph form.

CARBOHYDRATES

1. "Simple" carbohydrates constitute many different sugars.
   "Simple" carbohydrates exist in many food products.

2. Chemically, sugars consist of one or two small sugar molecules.
   Sugars supply quick energy to the body.

3. Cereals, fruits, and even milk contain different kinds of sugar.
   Cereals, fruits, and even milk provide the energy our bodies need to stay alive.

4. Table sugar contains sucrose.
   Table sugar satisfies a large part of our daily energy needs.

5. Fruits have a sugar called fructose.
   Fruits offer an alternative source of energy.

6. The kind of sugar found is milk is called lactose.
   Most people don't even realize that milk contains sugar.

7. Starch and related carbohydrates contain "complex" carbohydrates.
   Starch and related carbohydrates exist naturally in vegetables and grains.

8. They differ from simple carbohydrates.
   They consist of long chains of sugar molecules chemically bonded together.

9. The body uses complex carbohydrates less rapidly.
   The body takes more time to digest complex carbohydrates.

10. The human body needs both "simple" and "complex" carbohydrates.
    The human body must get both kinds in order to function as it should.

Assignment 3:B

If possible, combine each of the following groups of two sentences into one sentence each by making a half-sentence of one of the sentences and then attaching it to the other. Then write the combined sentences in paragraph form.

A DANGEROUS DRIVE

1. I usually enjoy a drive in the country.
   I consider myself a good driver.

2. The experience I had yesterday made me want to never go out on the highway again.
   The experience I had yesterday nearly cost me my life.

3. I went for a drive in the country.
   I enjoyed the scenery.

4. A large truck in front of me blocked my view.
   I couldn't see the road ahead very well.

5. A car approached from the opposite direction.
   A car came around a curve.

6. Suddenly, a motorcycle pulled out from behind the car.
   A motorcycle accelerated and started to pass the car.

7. The motorcycle moved to our side of the road.
   The motorcycle came directly toward us.

8. The motorcycle driver approached the truck and my car at a fantastic speed.
   The motorcycle driver didn't seem to notice us.

9. The driver of the truck stomped on his brakes.
    He honked his horn and swerved out of the motorcycle's way.

10. I nearly hit the back of the truck.
    I stopped my car just in time.

11. The motorcycle driver zoomed past us at a tremendous speed.
    The motorcycle driver didn't even turn back to look at us.

12. I look back on the experience now.
    I realize that there are many drivers like the one on the motorcycle.

13. I know that there are nuts like that on the road.
    I hesitate to risk my life driving.

Assignment 3:C

If possible, combine each of the following groups of two sentences into one sentence each by making a half-sentence of one of the sentences and then attaching it to the other. Then write the combined sentences in paragraph form.

NORMAN ROCKWELL

1. Most people in the United States understand little about art or artists.
    Most people in the United States can still recognize and enjoy the artwork of Norman Rockwell.

2. Rockwell grew up in and around New York City.
    Rockwell discovered and developed his tremendous talent for realistic illustration as a young man.

3. Rockwell sold his first cover illustration to *The Saturday Evening Post* when he was twenty-two years old.
    Rockwell never lacked work after that.

4. Rockwell painted over three hundred cover illustrations for *The Saturday Evening Post.*
    Rockwell's fame grew because of the work he did for that widely circulated magazine.

5. Rockwell took little time off from work.
    Rockwell worked every day of the year except Christmas.

6. Rockwell referred to himself as an illustrator rather than an artist.
    Rockwell didn't try to be a Picasso.

7. Rockwell commented on the subjects he chose to paint.
    Rockwell once said that he painted the world as he wanted it to be.

8. Rockwell's art remains today as a cultural testimony of the times he lived in.
   Rockwell's art depicts many of the social issues which were important in the United States during his lifetime.

9. Rockwell's paintings made him the most famous American illustrator of his era.
   Rockwell's paintings created a portrait of America that millions of people loved.

4.   SUBJECT AND OBJECT THE SAME

When the subject of one sentence is the **object** of another, the half-sentence method of combining may be used.

The sentence with the noun in common used as the **subject** always becomes the **half-sentence.** The sentence with the noun in common used as an **object** must be the **main** sentence.

The half-sentence follows the object of the main sentence. It does not precede it.

Example:

>I saw the dog.
>The dog was wagging its tail.
>>I saw the dog wagging its tail.

With some verbs sentences combined in this way may be ambiguous. They may be confusing to the reader because there are two possible meanings.

Example:

>I saw the dog.
>The dog was walking down the street.
>>I saw the dog walking down the street.
>>>(It is not clear who or what is walking down the street.)

When the object of a sentence is the subject of a passive sentence (which becomes the half-sentence), there is no problem with ambiguity.

Examples:

>Everyone listened to the band.
>The band was led by the new director.
>>Everyone listened to the band led by the new director.

>We always enjoy bread.
>Bread is baked by my mother.
>>We always enjoy bread baked by my mother.

Assignment 4:A

If possible, combine each of the following groups of two sentences into a single sentence each by making a half-sentence of one of the sentences and then attaching it to the other. Then write the combined sentences in paragraph form.

THE NOBEL PRIZE

1. Alfred Bernhard Nobel was born in 1833.
    Alfred Bernhard Nobel was a Swedish chemist and inventor.

2. Nobel experimented with nitroglycerine in order to find a safer explosive.
    Nobel perfected a combination of nitroglycerine and diatomaceous earth.
    The combination of nitroglycerine and diatomaceous earth was called dynamite.

3. Nobel was inclined toward pacifism.
    Nobel was unhappy with the use of his inventions.

4. He made a fortune from his inventions.
    He left his money in a funded foundation.

5. The interest from this fund was given as awards.
    The awards were for the promotion of international peace.

6. The Nobel Foundation gives awards for work in physics, chemistry, physiology, medicine, and peace-making efforts.
    The awards are called Nobel Prizes.

7. A Nobel Prize consists of a gold medal, a sum of money, and a diploma.
    A Nobel Prize is awarded without regard to nationality.

8. The prizes are given on December tenth of each year.
    December tenth is the anniversary of Nobel's death.

Assignment 4:B

If possible, combine each of the following groups of two or more sentences into a single sentence each by making a half-sentence of one or more of the sentences and then attaching it to the other. Then write the combined sentences in paragraph form.

THE COLONIZATION OF SPACE

1. People have many fantastic dreams.
    The dreams concern man's future.

2. One popular idea about the future predicts space colonies.
    The space colonies revolve around the earth.

3. Initially the space colonies will be able to sustain only a few dozen workers at a time.
    The space colonies will eventually expand in size and increase in comfort to the point where up to 50,000 people will live together in space.

4. The space colonies will feature carefully controlled environments for the people who inhabit them.
    The space colonies will be pleasant places to live and work.

5. The colonies' habitats will include swimming pools, artificial rivers, and comfortable apartments.
    The comfortable apartments will overlook pest-free, climate-controlled gardens.

6. They will receive solar energy.
    The solar energy will be reflected toward the colony by huge mirrors.

7. The colonies will be shaped like giant wheels.
    The colonies will spin to produce centrifugal force.
    The centrifugal force will simulate earth's gravity.

8. Many scientists imagine that the space colonies will be mini-utopias.
    Many scientists look forward to these future space colonies.

9. Some critics of this utopian dream point out that this space colony plan does not take into account man's social problems.
    Some critics of this utopian dream say it will never succeed.

10. They look at progress in another way.
    They believe that man should solve the problems of his society on earth instead of simply transplanting them to outer space.

Assignment 4:C

If possible, combine each of the following groups of two or more sentences into a single sentence each by making a half-sentence of one or more of the sentences and then attaching it to the other. Then write the combined sentences in paragraph form.

LANGUAGE ACQUISITION BY APES

1. A number of experiments have been conducted in recent years.
   These experiments deal with teaching language to animals.

2. Most of the experiments use apes.
   The apes live in human-like conditions.

3. Often the apes have human "parents."
   Their human "parents" work with them constantly.

4. Linguists assume that some apes possess the intelligence for language but lack the necessary vocal equipment.
   Linguists have developed several different ways for the apes to "talk" without speaking.

5. One experiment used colored plastic shapes as substitutes for spoken words.
   One experiment succeeded in teaching a chimpanzee to communicate with her trainers.
   The chimpanzee was named Sarah.

6. Another experiment provided a chimpanzee with a special, color-coded computer keyboard.
   It learned to communicate with humans by punching the correct keys.

7. Another experiment used gorillas instead of chimpanzees.
   In another experiment people have taught American Sign Language to these great apes.
   American Sign Language is normally used for communication between deaf people.

8. The language ability of these apes is not equal to that of humans.
   The language ability of these apes is still amazing.

5. COMPOUND HALF-SENTENCES

Two or more half-sentences may be compounded with *and, or, but,* or *yet* and attached to the same main sentence.

Examples:

> John was walking to school this morning.
> John noticed the cherry trees were blooming.
> John knew that spring had arrived.
> 1. Walking to school this morning and noticing the cherry trees were blooming, John knew that spring had arrived.
> 2. John, walking to school this morning and noticing the cherry trees were blooming, knew that spring had arrived.
>
> Mary felt tired.
> Mary was determined to finish the job.
> Mary continued working.
> 1. Feeling tired yet determined to finish the job, Mary continued working.
> 2. Mary, feeling tired yet determined to finish the job, continued working.

6. SUBORDINATORS AND PREPOSITIONS WITH HALF-SENTENCES

6.1   Time subordinators such as *while, when, after, before,* etc. may be placed at the front of half-sentences beinning with -*ing* verb forms.

Examples:

> While running down the street, George was attacked by a dog.
> When writing English, one should think about both form and meaning.
> After winning the game, the team was happy.

6.2   The contrast subordinator *although* can be used with **d-t-n forms** in some half-sentences.

Example:

> Although beaten by their rivals, the home team was not discouraged.

6.3   Certain **prepositions** such as *by, for, in, on,* and *upon* may also be placed at the front of half-sentences beginning with -*ing* verb forms.

Examples:

> By working hard, Albert got a promotion.
> For settling the dispute, Henry received the Nobel Peace Prize.
> In studying for the test, students must use their textbooks.
> On (upon) entering the room, George smelled smoke.

7. VARIETY IN WRITING

A number of sentence transforming and combining methods have been presented in the last four chapters:

> Passive Transformation (Chapter 9)
> Compounds (Chapter 10)
> Subordinate clauses and Relative clauses (Chapter 11)
> Half-sentences (Chapter 12)

Good writing in English requires a **variety** of

1. basic sentence patterns (Chapter 7),
2. types of sentence combinations (some compounds, some clauses, and some half-sentences), and
3. sentence length (some short sentences and some long sentences).

Notice the variety of sentence combinations in the following passage:

THE SEMINOLE WARS

On Christmas morning, 1837, the Seminoles and Miccosukees joined forces for one last desperate attempt to turn
    compound subject
back the United States troops. In a fierce battle which occurred near Lake Okeechobee, the Indians were driven
                                           relative clause
off by soldiers led by Zachary Taylor. They left many casualties on the United States side before they fled into the
                 half-sentence   subordinate clause
sanctuary of the Everglades.

   This was the last major encounter of the Second Seminole War although the bloody fighting continued
                                                                       subordinate clause
sporadically. On August 14, 1842 the war ended. Taking the lives of nearly 1,500 field troops and probably as
                                                              half-sentence
many Indians, this war cost the United States about $20 million.

   In 1848, a band of some 360 Indians remaining in Florida were goaded into an uprising that has been given
                                        half-sentence
the exaggerated title of the Third Seminole War. Aging Chief Billy Bowlegs was the leader of about 120 warriors
               relative clause
engaged in the rebellion. After a series of minor skirmishes which occurred in Central and South Florida, the
    half-sentence   relative clause
                                                            subordinate clause
Indians were subdued and repatriation to the West went on as usual. Ten years later the majority of the Indians
             compound predicate
had been removed and only a determined few who had fled deep into the Everglades remained in Florida. By 1908
    compound sentences   relative clause
the Seminoles living in Florida numbered about 275.
               half-sentence

Assignment 7:A

Combine the sentences below using a variety of methods. First, rearrange the sentences so that related sentences are near each other. Then combine them using the various methods presented in Chapters 9 through 12. Write your sentences in paragraph form.

THE BASTILLE

The Bastille was in France.

The Bastille was one of the most famous prisons in the world.

The Bastille was originally a fortress.

The Bastille was located in the heart of Paris.

Later the Bastille was turned into a prison.

Those who offended the King of France were imprisoned in the Bastille.

Many political prisoners spent their whole lives in the Bastille.

No sunlight reached the cells in the Bastille.

No sunlight reached the prisoners.

The prisoners in the Bastille were liberated in the French Revolution.

The Bastille was stormed by the people of Paris.

The people stormed the Bastille during the French Revolution.

The people released the prisoners.

The people completely demolished the Bastille.

The Bastille was a hated symbol of oppression.

Assignment 7:B

Combine the sentences below using a variety of methods. First, rearrange the sentences so that related sentences are near each other. Then combine them using the various methods presented in Chapters 9 through 12. Write your sentences in paragraph form.

PERCEPTION

No two people see things exactly alike.

The exact same image may be reproduced upon the retina of the eye.

The brain recalls past experience.

The brain interprets that image.

An Eskimo is exposed to very few very colorful flowers.

A Polynesian is exposed to many very colorful flowers.

A flower seems very brilliant to an Eskimo.

A flower may appear very pale to a Polynesian.

Artists see the same thing.

Artists react differently.

Artists interpret what they see in their paintings.

An artist's aim is to create a visual image.

An artist projects his interpretation in his pictures.

Assignment 7:C

Combine the sentences below using a variety of methods. First, rearrange the sentences so that related sentences are near each other. Then combine them using the various methods presented in Chapters 9 through 12. Write your sentences in paragraph form.

RIGHT-SIDE-UPNESS

Many things considered natural or normal are learned.

From birth, man feels his feet on the ground.

From birth, man feels the pull of gravity from below.

He reaches up with his hands to get things.

He reaches down with his hands to pick up things.

"Upness" seems part of his nature.

"Downness" seems part of his nature.

A series of experiments shows this is not so.

Some special eyeglasses were invented by scientists.

Some special eyeglasses turned everything upside down.

Scientists wanted to test "up-side-downness."

Volunteers wore these eyeglasses all the time.

Volunteers became completely disoriented.

They reached up to tie their shoelaces.

They stepped down to try to go up stairs.

They had no coordination.

At first, some had to crawl to get across a room.

After a while they got along comfortably with the glasses.

They were able to ride bicycles.

They were able to ski.

Up-side-downness eventually seemed right to them.

They lived normal lives.

After several weeks the glasses were taken off.

The volunteers were again completely disoriented.

The volunteers had to go through another period of adjustment.

Right-side-upness is learned in infancy.

Right-side-upness is reinforced through life.

Assignment 7.1:A

Write at least twenty basic sentences of your own on the topic of **pets.** *Combine these sentences using any of the methods that have been presented up to this point. Write your sentences in paragraph form.*

Assignment 7.1:B

Write at least twenty basic sentences of your own on the topic of **wild animals.** *Combine these sentences using any of the methods that have been presented up to this point. Write your sentences in paragraph form.*

Assignment 7.1:C

Write at least twenty basic sentences of your own on the topic of **farm animals.** *Combine these sentences using any of the methods that have been presented up to this point. Write your sentences in paragraph form.*

13
NOUN CLAUSES AND PHRASES

1. NOUN CLAUSES WITH INTRODUCERS

It is possible for a complete sentence to take the place of a noun. This is done by placing a function word called an **introducer** in front of the sentence. The addition of this function word changes the sentence into a noun clause.

A noun clause may be used as a subject, an object, or a complement in another sentence. The subject noun clause is always **singular** even though it may contain compound or plural nouns.

Here are some common **introducers**. They are used to change sentences into noun clauses:

that	if
how	whether or not
why	whether . . . (or not)
whichever	wherever

Examples:

Basic Sentences	Combined Sentences

He passed the test.
(*Something*) surprised his teacher.
    (subject)
	That he passed the test surprised his teacher.
	    (subject)

He passed the test.
I don't know (*something*).
            (object)
	I don't know *how he passed the test.*
	            (object)

He passed the test.
It appears (*something*).
        (complement)
	It appears *that he has passed the test.*
	        (complement)

76

Noun clauses may be used in any basic sentence pattern (these are explained in Chapter 7), but only the introducer with the right meaning should be used.

Examples:

Sentence pattern No. 1 S-V-O	*That he refuses to work* affects everyone. (subject)
Sentence pattern No. 2 S-V	*Whether George goes or stays* doesn't matter. (subject)
Sentence pattern No. 3 S-V$_L$-C	*That he passed the test* seems impossible. (subject) It seems *that I have failed the test.* (complement)
Sentence pattern No. 4 S-be-C	*Why I failed the test* is a mystery to me. (subject) The problem was *that I never studied.* (complement)

Assignment 1:A

Combine each of the following sets of sentences by making one into a noun clause and then writing it as the subject, object, or complement of the other in place of the (something). *Write your combined sentences in paragraph form.*

SELF-EDUCATION

1. It is not always necessary to have a formal education to become well-educated.
   (Something) is a recognized fact.

2. The person who reads a variety of books, magazines, and newspapers can become well-educated.
   (Something) is a recognized fact.

3. A person does or does not educate himself.
   (Something) depends on his motivation to improve.

4. People react to situations.
   (Something) can teach lessons about human behavior.

5. A person can learn from his mistakes if he wants to.
   (Something) is widely recognized.

6. We use the information available to us.
   (Something) determines how well we learn from our experiences.

7. We take advantage of the opportunities to learn.
   (Something) is all up to us.

Assignment 1:B

Combine each of the following sets of sentences by making one into a noun clause and then writing it as the subject, object, or complement of the other in place of the (something). *Write your combined sentences in paragraph form.*

COMPETITION: MENTAL VS. PHYSICAL

1. People like to play in competition.
   (Something) depends on the type of the game.

2. Some people like active sports.
   (Something) is a mystery to me.

3. Anyone would like to get battered and bruised in a football game.
   (Something) seems incredible to me.

4. Pros do it for money.
   (Something) is understandable.

5. Anyone can enjoy getting physically tackled and thrown around.
   I don't see (something).

6. Anyone who plays football for fun deserves all the battering he gets.
   I feel (something).

7. People match wits in intellectual competition.
   On the other hand, I can understand (something).

8. I enjoy mental rather than physical activity.
   (Something) is readily apparent.

Assignment 1:C

Combine each of the following sets of sentences by making one into a noun clause and then writing it as the subject, object, or complement of the other in place of the (something). Write your combined sentences in paragraph form.

POLYNESIAN NAVIGATORS

1. Few people realize (something).
    Some of the finest navigators in the history of the world were the early Polynesians.

2. Most modern Polynesians have forgotten (something).
    Their ancestors used the stars and ocean currents to sail across the wide Pacific Ocean without getting lost.

3. (Something) seems impossible.
    Ancient Polynesian navigators could sail from island to island across thousands of miles of ocean without technical instruments to guide them.

4. Many signs in the sky and the sea told the ancient Polynesians (something).
    They were on course or not.

5. Ancient Polynesian sailors knew (something).
    Certain cloud formations indicated the presence of an island.

6. Ocean current and swell patterns could tell them (something).
    They were going the right direction or sailing around in circles.

7. A pale green light reflected onto the underside of a cloud revealed (something).
    A low lying atoll whose shallow lagoon reflected the light was beneath the cloud.

8. The positions of numerous rising and setting stars on the horizon let the navigator know (something).
   He was sailing in the right direction.

9. Many modern Polynesians find it hard to explain (something).
   The art of navigating has been nearly completely lost among them.

10. (Something) is fortunate.
    The navigating art has been preserved by a few individuals.

2. NOUN CLAUSES AND DUMMY SUBJECTS

2.1   When a long noun clause introduced by *that* is used as the **subject** of a sentence, it is normally put after the predicate (but before any end shifters).

When this is done the **dummy subject** *it* (explained in Chapter 3) is placed in the normal subject position (after any front shifters).

The dummy subject *it* is always **singular.**

Example:

> *That he loves her with all his heart* is obvious.
>   noun clause

> *It* is obvious *that he loves her with all his heart.*
>   noun clause

2.2   When a noun clause introduced by *that* is used as the object or complement of a sentence, the introducer *that* may sometimes be left out. However, caution should be exercised, as omitting the *that* may result in confusion.

Examples:

> It appears *that we have lost the ball game.*
>   noun phrase (complement)

> It appears *we have lost the ball game.*
>   noun phrase (complement)

> I didn't know *that he was your uncle.*
>   noun phrase (object)

> I didn't know *he was your uncle.*
>   noun phrase (object)

Assignment 2:A

Rewrite each of the following sentences by using the dummy subject it *and placing the noun clause later in the sentence. Write your new sentences in paragraph form.*

IDENTIFICATION TAGS

1. That so many unknown soldiers have died and been buried in nameless graves seems sad.

2. That the United States armed forces issue metal identification tags to every soldier as part of his equipment is standard procedure.

3. That soldiers call these identification discs "dog tags" is common knowledge.

4. That soldiers wear these tags at all times is mandatory.

5. That at one time a soldier had to furnish his own identification tag if he wanted one seems strange to us.

6. However, that soldiers, even in combat, were not required to wear identification tags during the Civil War is not widely known.

7. That before dangerous battles soldiers often pinned pieces of paper with their names written on them so they could be identified if killed has been documented.

8. That every individual should have an identifiable number tatoo rather than a tag for positive identification has been suggested.

Assignment 2:B

Rewrite each of the following sentences by using the dummy subject it *and placing the noun clause later in the sentence. Write your new sentences in paragraph form.*

TWIN LANGUAGE

1. That children learn language by imitating their parents has long been thought.

2. That young children must have a model to pattern their own language after has been assumed.

3. That these ideas are true or false has been difficult to demonstrate.

4. However, a few years ago, that two young twins invented their own language amazed the world.

5. That they were the only ones who understood their unique language surprised everyone.

6. At first, that they were only babbling and not truly communicating was suspected.

7. Later, that the sounds they made to each other were a true language was demonstrated.

8. That their language was not related to any other human language on earth astounded investigating linguists and psychologists.

9. That in the absence of contact with adult language the two young girls had created their own language became apparent.

10. Although it was unbelievable, that they had truly done it without a model or adult help could not be denied.

Assignment 2:C

Rewrite each of the following sentences by using the dummy subject it *and placing the noun clause later in the sentence. Write your new sentences in paragraph form.*

THE DEAD SEA SCROLLS

1. That they were making one of the most important manuscript discoveries of modern times was not suspected by the Bedouins who entered a cave near the shore of the Dead Sea in 1947.

2. That what they would find in the cave would throw a blinding new light on scholars' interpretations of the Old and New Testaments didn't even occur to them.

3. That they were merely treasure hunters and didn't follow proper archaeological procedures is lamentable.

4. That trained archaeologists would have ever made the discovery is highly unlikely, however, because of the large number of unexplored caves in that area.

5. That some Bible scholars reacted to the scroll discovery with skepticism is understandable.

6. That the discovery was not a hoax soon became apparent.

7. At first, that the discovery would revolutionize scholarly thinking about Biblical history was not suspected.

8. As time went by, that the seven leather and two copper scrolls were of inestimable value was proven beyond doubt.

9. That there are no more archaeological surprises awaiting the world has not been proven.

10. That more such discoveries will be made in the future is very possible.

3.   NOUN CLAUSES WITH SUBSTITUTORS

3.1   Another way to make a noun clause is to use a function word called a **substitutor**.

The substitutor takes the place of the subject, the object, the complement, a demonstrative, or an adverb of the sentence used as the noun clause.

The following function words are used as **substitutors** in noun clauses:

who	(for human subjects)	when	(for time)
whoever	(for human subjects)	where	(for place)
whom	(for human objects)	whose	(for possessive nouns)
what	(for things)	which	(for a specific thing)
whatever	(for things)	why	(for reason)
how	(for manner)		

Although these substitutors look like the function words used to form wh- questions (Chapter 7, Section 11), noun clauses are not questions. Therefore, normal word order is used in noun clauses.

3.2   When a substitutor takes the place of a subject or possessive modifier, normal word order is followed.

Examples:

(*Somebody*) comes first.   (*Somebody*) gets the job.
   subject   subject

Whoever comes first (noun clause)
substitutor

Whoever comes first gets the job.
      noun clause

(*Somebody's*) homework hasn't been done.   The teacher wants to know (*something*).
  possessive   object

Whose homework hasn't been done (noun clause)
substitutor

The teacher wants to know *whose homework hasn't been done.*
                    noun clause

3.3   When a substitutor takes the place of an object, complement, or adverb, it is moved to the front of the noun clause. Except for this change, normal word order is followed (aux-words are not moved).

Examples:

The class will elect (*somebody*) president.   I wonder (*something*)
            object   object

The class will elect *whom* (noun clause)
          substitutor

Whom the class will elect (noun clause with substitutor moved to front)
substitutor

I wonder *whom the class will elect president.*
          noun clause

Your major is (something).   The counselor wants to know (*something*).
            complement   object

Your major is *what* (noun clause)
            substitutor

What your major is (noun clause with substitutor moved to front)
substitutor

The counselor wants to know *what your major is.*
                                            noun clause

John went (*somewhere*).   I don't know (*something*).
            adverb of place   object

John went *where* (noun clause)
            substitutor

Where John went (noun clause with substitutor moved to front)
substitutor

I don't know *where John went.*
                        noun clause

Additional examples:

I don't know *who won the game.* (subject substitutor)
                        noun clause (object)

Whatever happens to George affects all of us. (subject substitutor)
        noun clause (subject)

Robert told me *which girl he admired most.* (demonstrative substitutor)
                        noun clause (object)

I can't see *how the magician makes the girl disappear.* (adverb of manner substitutor)
                        noun clause (object)

I want to know *when he took the test.* (adverb of time substitutor)
                        noun clause (object)

Assignment 3:A

Rewrite one of each of the following pairs of sentences into a noun clause using a substitutor. Then combine it with the other sentence. Write all your combined sentences in paragraph form.

A STRANGE ENCOUNTER

1. My friend told me (something).
    A strange man came to her house last week (in some way).

2. She didn't know (something).
    He was (somebody).

3. She had no idea (of something).
    He had come from (somewhere).

4. She asked him (something).
    He needed (something).

5. She couldn't understand (something).
    He had come to her house (for some reason).

6. But she never found out (something) because he turned and walked away without saying a word.
    He wanted (something).

7. She didn't have any idea (of something).
    He went (somewhere).

8. He didn't tell her (something).
    He was going (somewhere).

9. He didn't even say (something).
   His name was (something).

10. She can still remember (something).
    He looked like (something).

11. She will never forget (something).
    He looked (in some way) desperate.

Assignment 3:B

Rewrite one of each of the following pairs of sentences into a noun clause using a substitutor. Then combine it with the other sentence. Write all your combined sentences in paragraph form.

STRANGE RECORDS

1. Recently I read (something).
   (In some way) people have established strange records.

2. I have often wondered (something).
   (Something) prompts people to do some strange things.

3. (Something) surprised me.
   I read (something).

4. (Somebody) played a violin solo underwater.
   (Somebody) probably couldn't decide whether to bathe or play music.

5. I wonder (something).
   (Something) made a man walk clear across the country from New York to San Francisco playing a violin all the way.

6. I pondered on (something).
   (Something) happened to the man who ate sixty-three bananas in ten minutes.

7. or (someone's) record was broken when a man downed fourteen eggs in one minute.

8. (Somebody) walked on his hands for 871 miles from Vienna to Paris.
   (Somebody) might have had foot troubles before this stunt,

9. but afterwards, I wonder (something).
   (Something) happened to his hands.

10. I have given up speculating on (something).
     (Something) may yet occur.

11. Still, a new edition of world records may tell me (something).
     Someone will have done (something) next.

Assignment 3:C

Rewrite one of each of the following pairs of sentences into a noun clause using a substitutor. Then combine it with the other sentence. Write all your sentences in paragraph form.

A CONFESSION

1. Nobody has any doubt about (something).
   It happened (somewhere).

2. Almost everybody knows (something).
   It happened (sometime).

3. Some have asked me (something).
   I did it (for some reason).

4. Others, more curious, ask me (something).
   I did it (in some way).

5. A few want to know (something).
   (Somebody) helped me.

6. I haven't told them (something).
   They want to know (something).

7. They don't know (something).
   I haven't told them (for some reason).

8. I really don't know (something).
   It happened (for some reason).

9. Nor do I know (something).
   It happened (in some way).

10. All I really know is (something).
    (Something) happened.

4.   NOUN PHRASES FROM PREDICATES

4.1   It is possible to use part of the predicate of a sentence as a noun phrase. Only predicates with *-ing* verb forms or with **base verb forms** can be used in this way.

1.   **Predicates with *-ing* verb forms.** The aux-word must be removed when used as a noun phrase.

        Someone / was   passing the test.
        (subject) (aux-word) (predicate with *-ing* verb form)

                    was / *passing the test*
                           noun phrase

2.   **Predicates with base verb forms.** The aux-word must be removed and the function word *to* is placed before the base form. (This is often called the **infinitive form.**)

        Someone / will   pass the test.
        (subject) (aux-word) (predicate with base form)

                    will / *pass the test*
                           noun phrase

Examples:

   Noun phrase as subject
      Passing the test worried John.
      To pass the test was his goal.

   Noun phrase as object of the verb
      John tried *passing the test.*
      John tried *to pass the test.*

   Noun phrase as object of the preposition
      John worried about *passing the test.*
      (*To* + base form cannot be used as the object of a preposition.)

   Noun phrase as complement
      John's goal is *passing the test.*
      John's goal is *to pass the test.*
      He seemed *to worry a lot.*
      (Most linking verbs cannot be followed by an *-ing* noun phrase.)

The *-ing* noun phrase can be modified by **adjectives and possessives.**

   His *passing the test* delighted John.
   (possessive)

   Brilliant *thinking* helped him on the test.
   (adjective)

4.2   Both *-ing* and *to* + base noun phrases may be used as **objects** of some verbs. However, **both types can not be used with all verbs.** Some verbs require the *-ing* form while others require the *to* + base form. (Appendix E, page 141, lists many of these verbs.)

Assignment 4:A

Write appropriate noun phrases *in place of the blanks in the sentences below. Write your sentences in paragraph form, remembering to keep the continuity of the paragraph.*

LEISURE TIME ACTIVITIES

1.   I enjoy _____ .

2.   However, I don't like _____ .

3.   In the summer, _____ is fun.

4.   But in the winter, it is impossible _____ .

5.   If I'm alone, I try _____ .

6.   When my friends are with me, we sometimes want _____ .

7.   At some time or another most of us have attempted _____ .

8.   We once agreed _____ .

9.   I have postponed _____ .

10.   However, at least once in my life, I hope _____ .

Assignment 4:B

Write appropriate noun phrases *in place of the blanks in the sentences below. Write your sentences in paragraph form, remembering to keep the continuity of the paragraph.*

MY VOCATION

1. When I was young, my mother wanted me _____ .

2. She hoped _____ .

3. But I didn't plan on _____ .

4. I considered _____ .

5. However, I reconsidered and decided _____ .

6. I agreed _____

7. and intended _____ .

8. I practiced _____ .

9. I forgot _____

10. although I meant _____ .

11. Now I want _____ .

12. I intend _____ .

13. I plan on _____ .

14. I expect _____ .

Assignment 4:C

Write appropriate noun phrases in place of the blanks in the sentences below. Write your sentences in paragraph form, remembering to keep the continuity of the paragraph.

A NEW SKILL

1. Last week I began _____ .

2. _____ wasn't easy.

3. I couldn't help _____ .

4. But I kept on _____ .

5. Finally, I started _____ .

6. I hoped _____ .

7. I didn't expect _____ .

8. However, I learned _____ .

9. After a while, I stopped _____ .

10. Then I missed _____ .

11. Today, I will continue _____ .

12. I plan on _____ .

5. NOUN PHRASES AND DUMMY SUBJECTS

The **dummy subject** *it* may also be used with noun phrases. However, only the *to* + base form can be used with the dummy subject *it*.

If *-ing* phrases are used as the original subject, they must be changed to the *to* + base form when the dummy subject *it* is used.

Example:

Enduring hardship and cold is the lot of an arctic explorer.
    noun phrase

It is the lot of an arctic explorer *to endure hardship and cold*.
                    noun phrase

Assignment 5:A

Rewrite each of the following sentences by using the dummy subject it *and placing the noun clause or phrase later in the sentence. Write your sentences in paragraph form.*

CITY VS. COUNTRY LIFE

1. That people like to live in a city is understandable.

2. On the other hand, that people like to live in the country is understandable also.

3. To see shows, attend concerts, participate in educational or political events, and eat in many different kinds of restaurants is a part of city life.

4. Enduring smog, noise, and crowds is also a part of city life.

5. That the country provides fresh air, a quiet peaceful atmosphere, and freedom from noxious traffic fumes cannot be denied.

6. Relaxing, jogging, hiking, and just plain loafing are great.

7. That some people, however, find life in the country monotonous is true.

8. That others find life in the city disturbing and unsettling is equally true.

9. Living in the city, but spending weekends and vacations in the country, seems to be the solution for many.

Assignment 5:B

Rewrite each of the following sentences by using the dummy subject it *and placing the noun clause or noun phrase later in the sentence. Write your sentences in paragraph form.*

MUSIC

1. That "music hath charms to calm the savage beast" is an old adage.

2. That listening to music can affect human and animal emotional states has been demonstrated.

3. To tap one's feet and sway rhythmically is natural when listening to music with a strong beat.

4. That soft dreamy music has a soothing effect and may often cause people to doze or sleep has been observed.

5. That some music, like much that occurs at rock concerts, can induce hypnotic states of frenzy, particularly in emotionally immature people, seems probable.

6. That playing martial music at political or recruitment rallies promotes patriotism is well known.

7. Playing mysterious and eerie music on the sound track of spine-chilling movies is a common practice, thus creating a mood for what follows.

8. Watching a wild western without the accompanying music would not be nearly as exciting.

9. Even during the silent era of early movies, playing appropriate piano or organ music was necessary to set the mood and create the proper atmosphere for the screenplay.

10. That a silent world would be a monotonous world cannot be denied.

Assignment 5:C

Rewrite each of the following sentences by using the dummy subject it *and placing the noun clause or noun phrase later in the sentence. Write your sentences in paragraph form.*

NUTRITION

1. That people need a balanced diet is a well known fact.

2. If people want to be healthy, eating foods from four basic food groups is necessary.

3. However, discovering this fact was not a simple task.

4. Once it was discovered, convincing people that it was true was an even greater job.

5. To change people's eating habits was a great challenge.

6. To convince English sailors that vitamin C from citrus fruit was necessary took much suffering and death from scurvy.

7. That people began to realize the value of vitamin D in their diet was not until after many thousands had been crippled by rickets.

8. Even today, getting people to change their dietary habits is not easy.

9. That adults cling to the customs they learned as children is obvious.

10. For example, even though brown rice is more nutritious than white rice, convincing people who think of it as animal feed that eating it would improve their health is extremely difficult.

6. COMPOUND NOUN CLAUSES CONNECTED WITH SUBORDINATORS

When using two or more noun clauses in a sentence, the time relationship of the **second** clause is shown by the time subordinator and **not** by the verb form.* The verb form in the second clause is either simple present or simple past, whichever is the established time.

Examples:

John said (that)
- he would study
- *while* (same time)
- his roommates *would be* at the game.

John said he would study *while* his roommates *were* at the game.

Joe expects (that)
- he will be elected student body president
- *when* (same time)
- he *will be* a senior a year from now.

Joe expects that he will be elected student body president *when* he *is* a senior a year from now.

Mary decided (that)
- she *would work*
- *after* (later time) or *before* (earlier time)
- she *would wash* her hair.

Mary decided that she *would work after* she *washed* her hair.

OR

Mary decided that she *would wash* her hair *before* she *worked.*

The president has assured the people (that)
- inflation *will be* controlled
- *after* or *before*
- he *will lower* taxes.

The president has assured the people that he *will lower* taxes *after* inflation *is* controlled.

OR

The president has assured the people that inflation *will be controlled before* he *lowers* taxes.

*In some cases, other non-time subordinators may be used (e.g., *so . . . that*)

Assignment 6:A

Combine the pairs of noun clauses in each sentence below using the time subordinator indicated. Then write the sentences in paragraph form. Be sure to change the verb form in the second clause.

TERRY'S AMBITION

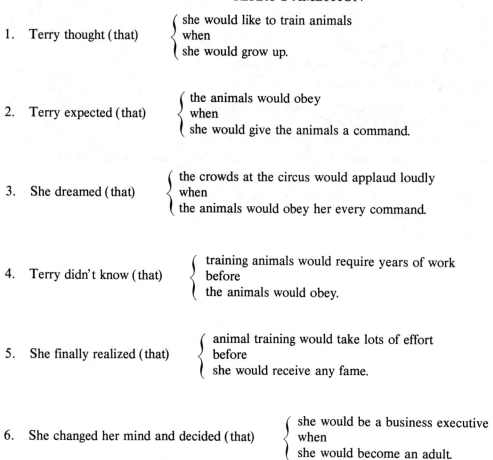

1. Terry thought (that)
    { she would like to train animals
    when
    she would grow up.

2. Terry expected (that)
    { the animals would obey
    when
    she would give the animals a command.

3. She dreamed (that)
    { the crowds at the circus would applaud loudly
    when
    the animals would obey her every command.

4. Terry didn't know (that)
    { training animals would require years of work
    before
    the animals would obey.

5. She finally realized (that)
    { animal training would take lots of effort
    before
    she would receive any fame.

6. She changed her mind and decided (that)
    { she would be a business executive
    when
    she would become an adult.

Assignment 6:B

Combine the pairs of noun clauses in each sentence below using the time subordinator indicated. Then, write the sentences in paragraph form. Be sure to change the verb form in the second clause.

SISTER KNOWS BEST

My brother and sister had an argument yesterday.

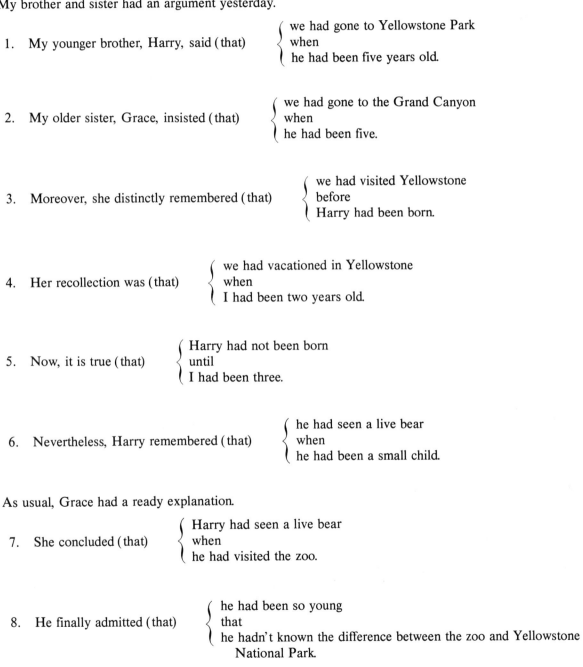

1. My younger brother, Harry, said (that)
    - we had gone to Yellowstone Park
    - when
    - he had been five years old.

2. My older sister, Grace, insisted (that)
    - we had gone to the Grand Canyon
    - when
    - he had been five.

3. Moreover, she distinctly remembered (that)
    - we had visited Yellowstone
    - before
    - Harry had been born.

4. Her recollection was (that)
    - we had vacationed in Yellowstone
    - when
    - I had been two years old.

5. Now, it is true (that)
    - Harry had not been born
    - until
    - I had been three.

6. Nevertheless, Harry remembered (that)
    - he had seen a live bear
    - when
    - he had been a small child.

As usual, Grace had a ready explanation.

7. She concluded (that)
    - Harry had seen a live bear
    - when
    - he had visited the zoo.

8. He finally admitted (that)
    - he had been so young
    - that
    - he hadn't known the difference between the zoo and Yellowstone National Park.

Assignment 6:C

Combine the pairs of noun clauses in each sentence below using the time subordinator indicated. Then write the sentences in paragraph form. Be sure to change the verb form in the second clause.

A FAMILY GARDEN

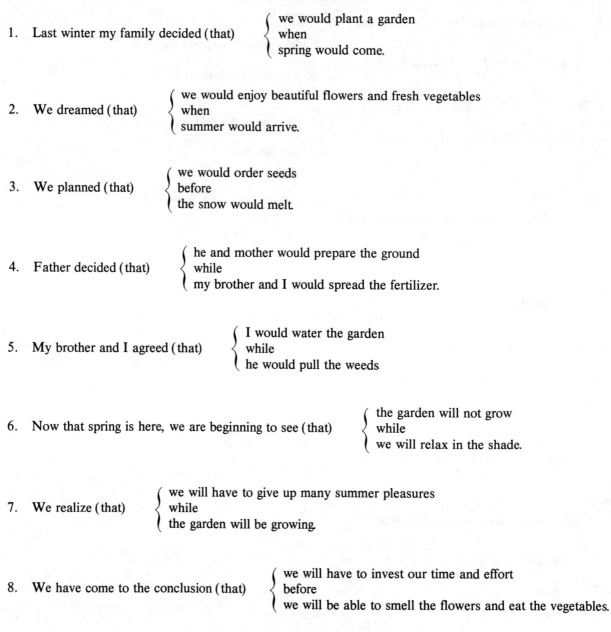

1. Last winter my family decided (that) { we would plant a garden / when / spring would come.

2. We dreamed (that) { we would enjoy beautiful flowers and fresh vegetables / when / summer would arrive.

3. We planned (that) { we would order seeds / before / the snow would melt.

4. Father decided (that) { he and mother would prepare the ground / while / my brother and I would spread the fertilizer.

5. My brother and I agreed (that) { I would water the garden / while / he would pull the weeds.

6. Now that spring is here, we are beginning to see (that) { the garden will not grow / while / we will relax in the shade.

7. We realize (that) { we will have to give up many summer pleasures / while / the garden will be growing.

8. We have come to the conclusion (that) { we will have to invest our time and effort / before / we will be able to smell the flowers and eat the vegetables.

Assignment 6.1:A

*Write at least twenty basic sentences on the topic of **exercise**. Combine these sentences into a short essay using any of the combining methods that have been presented.*

Assignment 6.1:B

*Write at least twenty basic sentences on the topic of **work**. Combine these sentences into a short essay using any of the combining methods that have presented.*

Assignment 6.1:C

*Write at least twenty basic sentences on the topic of **education**. Combine these sentences into a short essay using any of the combining methods that have been presented.*

14

ADDING INFORMATION

1. ADDING NON-ESSENTIAL INFORMATION

1.1 When one sentence contains information about a noun in another sentence, the two sentences may be combined. The information is added immediately after the noun.

This information may be in the form of

1. a noun (with or without modifiers),
2. a noun phrase, or half-sentence, or
3. a noun clause with a substitutor or a relative clause.

Both the subject of the extra information sentence and the noun which the extra information follows must be the same person or thing.

Examples:

James Tidwell performs many operations.
(extra information)→James Tidwell is a surgeon.
James Tidwell, a surgeon, performs many operations.

Seaweed contains many nutrients.
(extra information)→Seaweed is a product of the ocean.
Seaweed, a product of the ocean, contains many nutrients.

He was driven to compete fiercely by his main object.
(extra information)→His main objective in life was to become a millionaire.
He was driven to compete fiercely by his main object in life—to become a millionaire.

Their purpose was not realized.
(extra information)→Their purpose was passing the test.
Their purpose (passing the test) was not realized.

My mother is confined to a wheelchair.
(extra information)→My mother was injured in an accident last year.
My mother, who was injured in an accident last year, is confined to a wheelchair.

1.2 Notice that in the examples above, the identity of the noun that the extra information follows is clear without this added information. Therefore, this extra information is set off by punctuation marks.

Extra information added to a sentence may be set off in three different ways:

1. **Commas** are used when the information is closely related to the rest of the sentence.

    American Indians, the original inhabitants of the American continent, are very different from the people of India.

    The electric light bulb, invented by Thomas Edison, was first commercially produced in 1879.

2. **Dashes** are used when the extra information is not as closely related.

    American Indians—often called Amerindians—are very different from the people of India.

    The electric light bulb—an essential part of today's world—was first commercially produced in 1879.

3. **Parentheses** are used when the extra information is distantly related. Information which would not normally be a part of a sentence because of its distant relationship can be inserted between parentheses.

    American Indians (whom Mormons called Lamanites) are very different from the people of India.

    The electric light bulb (how could we live without it today?) was first commercially produced in 1879.

Assignment 1:A

Rewrite the following sentences by combining them. Add the extra information from one after the noun which is the same as the subject of the extra information sentence. Use commas, dashes, or parentheses.

AUSTRALIAN ANIMALS

1. Some of the earth's most unusual animals are found in Australia.
    Australia is a continent widely separated from the rest of the world.

2. Most people know that Australia is the home of the kangaroo.
    The kangaroo is a large animal which carries its young in a pouch.

3. They don't often know that baby kangaroos weigh less than an ounce when born.
    Baby kangaroos may grow to weigh over a hundred pounds as adults.

4. For many weeks, the baby kangaroo never leaves the security of its mother's pouch.
    The baby kangaroo is born blind and helpless.

5. The model for the "teddy bear" was the Australian koala bear.
    The koala bear is not really a bear at all.

6. Koala bears are extremely shy and gentle.
   Koala bears eat the leaves of the eucalyptus tree.

7. The platypus may be the strangest of them all.
   The platypus has webbed feet and a duck bill.

8. The platypus also has a tail like a beaver's.
   The platypus lives near water and is an excellent swimmer.

9. Surprisingly, the platypus lays eggs.
   The playtypus is covered with thick fur.

10. Other unusual animals are also found in Australia.
    Other unusual animals are the spiny anteater, the wallaby, the wombat, and the flying opossum.

Assignment 1:B

Rewrite the following sentences by combining them. Add the extra information from one after the noun which is the same as the subject of the extra information sentence. Use commas, dashes, or parentheses.

ILLEGAL ALIENS

1. Some people live in one country and work in another.
   One country is their homeland.

2. This is done legally or illegally.
   Illegally is without proper papers.

3. In the United States, illegal aliens are periodically sent back to their own countries.
   Illegal aliens are people who have no legal right to be in the country.

4. A "guesstimate" places the number of illegal aliens in the United States at between three million and five million.
   A "guesstimate" is an unofficial, undocumented estimate.

5. Borders are often long and hard to patrol.
   Borders are boundaries between countries.

6. Border communities provide excellent cover for the people who manage to cross the border illegally.
   Border communities are cities with thousands of legal immigrants.

7. Some illegal aliens return again and again to work in the United States.
   Illegal aliens are agricultural workers from Mexico and other countries.

8. Crimes are often linked to illegal immigration.
   Crimes are robbery and rape.

9. Charles Perez is a director for the Immigration and Naturalization Service that includes El Paso, Texas.
   Charles Perez contends that half of that city's downtown crime is related in some way to illegal immigration.

10. Employers are hirers of illegal immigrants.
    Employers are accused of abetting the problem.

11. As long as menial jobs pay ten times what a person can make at home, illegal immigration will remain a problem.
    Menial jobs are those which require little or no skills.

Assignment 1:C

Rewrite the following sentences by combining them. Add the extra information from one after the noun which is the same as the subject of the extra information sentence. Use commas, dashes, or parentheses.

REFUGEES

1. One big problem in the world today is displaced persons.
   Displaced persons are expatriates without a homeland.

2. Among these are refugees.
   Refugees have problems locating in a new land.

3. Refugees are without a country.
   Refugees are sometimes refused entry into countries to which they have fled.

4. Unlike the illegal alien, the refugee must seek asylum in another place.
   The illegal alien can return to his native land.

5. During rebellions, the losing leaders usually flee the country to avoid being jailed or put to death.
   Rebellions are internal strife within a country.

6. They must find refuge in another country.
   Another country is a neutral place.

7. During World War II, thousands of refugees were eventually relocated in Canada, the United States, and Australia.
   Thousands of refugees were Germans, Poles, Czechs, and other Europeans.

8. Before being legally accepted into the new countries, these refugees lived in displacement camps.
   Displacement camps are temporary barracks or shelters often surrounded by barbed wire.

9. & 10. Constant political upheaval has created a new world problem.
   Constant political upheaval is the overturning of governments.
   A new world problem is thousands and thousands of refugees.

2. ADDING ESSENTIAL INFORMATION

2.1   Sometimes nouns, noun phrases, or noun clauses added after a noun provide information which is necessary to the identity of the noun they follow.

When the added information is essential to the identity of the noun which it follows, it is **not** set off with commas, dashes, or parentheses.

Examples:

> Elizabeth *the First* felt that Mary *Queen of Scots* was a threat and had her executed.
> The picture *hanging above the fireplace* is an original oil painting.
> All the students *who fail this class* must take it again.

2.2   A good test to determine if the information is or is not vital (whether commas, dashes or parentheses should be used) is to take it out. If the identity of the noun remains clear, then the added information is not necessary and should be set off. If the noun is not clearly identified when the information is removed, commas, dashes, or parentheses should not be used since the information is necessary.

In the examples below, whether or not commas, dashes, or parentheses are used depends on the situation.

Examples:

> My brother, Tom, will be here tonight. (I have only one brother named Tom.)
> My brother Tom will be here tonight. (I have more than one brother.)
>
> The girl, standing near the window, is my cousin. (There is only one girl in the room.)
> The girl standing near the window is my cousin. (There is more than one girl in the room but only one near the window.)
>
> The students (who came late) missed the quiz. (All of the students we are talking about came late.)
> The students who came late missed the quiz. (Some of the students came late.)

Assignment 2.3:A

Copy the passage below, inserting commas, dashes, or parentheses where necessary.

LANGUAGE

My native language English is the most sensible language of all. The grammar is logical and the vocabulary sensible. This is not true of other languages such as Farsi German or Finnish. They seem to me a monolingual speaker of English to be illogical and senseless. All students who study English do not feel the way I do. Some students who are always translating from their own languages feel that English cannot possibly be learned. These students who speak their native languages at all times seem to find no logical order in English grammar. The students who try to speak and write exclusively in English seem to do much better. They have finally realized that any language Japanese French or Samoan has its own language structure which must be used as one speaks or writes the words of that tongue. A language whatever it is is sensible and logical to the native speaker who has learned that language as part of the maturation process. Somehow one internalizes sound differences and grammatical rules as he acquires the vocabulary of his native language.

Assignment 2.3:B

Copy the passage below, inserting commas, dashes, or parentheses where necessary.

"PEANUTS"

"Peanuts" a famous American cartoon strip was created by Charles Schulz over fifteen years ago. Schulz called Sparky by his friends has created many characters for his internationally known cartoon strip.

Charlie Brown one of the original "Peanuts" characters is a boy who never wins. Charlie Brown's dog Snoopy is perhaps the most widely known character from the cartoon strip. Snoopy who plays tennis and ice hockey has many human traits. Charlie Brown suffers a lot because of what Lucy a neighbor girl does to him. Lucy in turn suffers because Schroeder a boy who devotes himself to playing Beethoven on a small piano never returns her attention. Charlie Brown's sister Sally is a more recent addition to the strip. Many sports-minded readers of the strip enjoy Peppermint Patty a top athlete but a sleepy student. Snoopy's frequent companion Woodstock is a tiny bird who types and takes dictation. Linus the favorite of many "Peanuts" readers always carries a security blanket as he waits for the "Great Pumpkin" on Halloween.

"Peanuts" cartoons written originally for a United States audience have been translated into many languages and distributed internationally. Charlie Brown and his dog Snoopy are probably as well known as the President of the United States. The greatest tribute to "Peanuts" popularity and Schulz's success as a cartoonist probably came when the U.S. spaceships which went to the moon were named Snoopy and Charlie Brown.

Assignment 2.3:C

Copy the passage below, inserting commas, dashes, or parentheses where necessary.

HOMECOMING

Homecoming with its parades queens and ballgames is a big event on college campuses. Most homecoming weeks are held in the fall the traditional good-will season. The alumni students of bygone years speak nostalgically of the good old days. Sports fans who turn out in large numbers to help celebrate are especially enthusiastic at the football game. The football players heroes if they win the game villains if they don't try their hardest to beat the other team their most bitter rivals. The queen who reigns over the activities is usually elected by the student body. Her attendants all of whom were finalists in the queen contest are also feted. Schools try hard to impress visitors who may later make large financial contributions to the institution. After the week is over academics which take a back seat during Homecoming become primary once again.

Assignment 2.1:A

Supply additional information for each of the sentences below. Rewrite the sentences in paragraph form, placing the new information in the space between the commas. If the information you add is essential, leave the commas out.

CONTINENTS

1. The world's continents, _____ , are very different.

2. Africa, _____ , has an area of nearly twelve million square miles and has over 350 million people.

3. Asia, _____ , has approximately two and one-half billion people in its seventeen million square miles.

4. Antarctica, _____ , has no permanent human population on its five and one-half million square miles of land.

5. Europe, _____ , has over 650 million people but less than four million square miles of land.

6. Australia, _____ , has a population of only about thirteen million and an area of nearly three million square miles.

7. North America, _____ , has a population approaching 350 million and an area of 9.4 million square miles.

8. South America, _____ , has almost two hundred million people and an area of 6,880,000 square miles.

9. Sometimes considered a continent, Oceania, _____ , has a population of a little over one million and an area of over three million square miles scattered among 25,000 islands.

Assignment 2.1:B

Supply additional information for each of the sentences below. Rewrite the sentences in paragraph form, placing the new information in the space between the commas. If the information you add is essential, leave the commas out.

THE SOLAR SYSTEM

1. The planets of our solar system revolve around the sun, _____ .

2. Mercury, _____ , is the closest planet to the sun.

3. Venus, _____ , is Earth's closest neighbor.

4. We, of course, live on the earth, _____ .

5. For many years earthlings have dreamed of traveling to Mars, _____ .

6. Jupiter, _____ , has twelve moons.

7. Saturn, _____ , is the second largest planet.

8. After Saturn comes Uranus, _____ .

9. Neptune, _____ , takes 165 earth years to revolve around the sun.

10. The ninth planet is Pluto, _____ .

Assignment 2.1:C

Supply additional information for each of the sentences below. Rewrite the sentences in paragraph form, placing the new information in the space between the commas. If the information you add is essential, leave the commas out.

INVENTORS

1. Our lives have been made more productive through the efforts of inventors, _____ .

2. Johann Guttenberg, _____ , is believed to have been the first European to print with movable type.

3. Benjamin Franklin, _____ , is responsible for bifocal glasses, the lightening rod, and the stove which bears his name.

4. Samuel B. Morse, _____ , was responsible for telegraphy, including the code of dots and dashes.

5. Alfred Nobel, _____ , invented dynamite.

6. Alexander Graham Bell, _____ , conceived the idea of transmitting speech by electricity and gave us the telephone.

7. Thomas Alva Edison, _____ , invented such things as wax paper, the mimeograph, the phonograph, storage batteries, and 1089 other things.

8. Guglielmo Marconi, _____ , developed the wireless telegraph, the forerunner of today's radios.

9. Orville and Wilbur Wright, _____ , made the first flight in a power driven airplane.

10. Robert H. Goddard, _____ , completed and successfully fired the world's first liquid fuel rocket.

Assignment 2.2:A

Write at least twenty related sentences about **modes of travel.** *Then add non-essential information to at least ten of your sentences.*

Assignment 2.2:B

Write at least twenty related sentences about **war** *or* **wars.** *Then add non-essential information to at least ten of your sentences.*

Assignment 2.2:C

Write at least twenty related sentences about **works of art.** *Then add non-essential information to at least ten of your sentences.*

15

TRANSITION WORDS
AND VARIETY IN WRITING

1. TRANSITION WORDS

1.1   Sentences are seldom used in isolation. In writing, related sentences are usually grouped together in paragraphs.

Relationships between sentences within paragraphs are often shown by transition words and phrases. These do **not connect sentences**—they are part of one sentence and indicate its relationship to the preceding sentence or sentences.

1.2   A number of different transition words or phrases may be used. The choice depends on the relationships between the sentences. In the list below, the more common transition words and phrases are grouped according to general meaning. Nevertheless, many have specific meanings—all the transition words or phrases within a category do not have exactly the same meaning. Therefore, they cannot always be freely substituted for one another.

Difference or Contrast	Reason or Result	Time or Sequence
but	accordingly	earlier
conversely	as a consequence	finally
however*	as a result	first, second, etc.
instead*	consequently*	in the first place
nevertheless*	for this (that) reason	later
on the contrary*	hence	meanwhile
on the other hand*	therefore*	next
otherwise	thus	now
still		then
yet		

Example or Illustration	Emphasis or Clarification	Additional Information
as a matter of fact*	after all	also
for example	anyway	by the way*
for instance	at any rate	furthermore
in fact*	at least	in addition
namely	indeed	incidentally*
that is	in fact*	likewise
	in other words*	moreover
	of course*	
	to be sure*	

*May be placed at any junction of sentence units (see 1.4 below).

1.3   Some of these transition expressions may be used for more than one purpose:

Example:

Samoa has beautiful, tropical scenery. Incidentally, it also has a lot of mosquitoes.

In this case, *incidentally* introduces **additional** information which is in **contrast** with the pleasant tone of the first sentence.

1.4   Generally, transition words or phrases are set off by commas and are placed at the beginning of a sentence. However, some of them (those marked by an asterisk in the list above) may be placed at any junction of sentence units—between a front shifter and a subject, between a subject and a predicate, and between the predicate and an end shifter. Within the predicate they may also be placed between the first aux-word and the following verb (or timeless aux-word).

Examples:

The platypus, which lives in Tasmania and Australia, lays eggs.
However, it is classified as a mammal because it has mammary glands.

The second sentence could also be written in three other ways:

It, however, is classified as a mammal because it has mammary glands.
It is, however, classified as a mammal because it has mammary glands.
It is classified as a mammal, however, because it has mammary glands.

The platypus belongs to a very small group of primitive mammals.
As a matter of fact, the spiny anteater is the only other animal in the group.

The second sentence could also be written in two other ways:

The spiny anteater, as a matter of fact, is the only other animal in the group.
The spiny anteater is, as a matter of fact, the only other animal in the group.

Assignment 1:A

List all of the transition words in the passage below by sentence number. Then label each one according to the relationship between sentences (i.e., contrast, time, reason, etc.) which it shows.

THE GUINNESS BOOK OF WORLD RECORDS

[1] The first *Guinness Book of World Records* appeared in 1956. [2] The McWhirter brothers, at this time, were not inundated by people's requests to get their names in the book. [3] The authors, consequently, did considerable research to find the facts to include in their book. [4] Today status seekers even invent new items or events to get their

names into this book. [5]Still, it is not easy to get into the Guinness Book of Records. [6]It can be done, however. [7]In the first place, one must have actual proof of his record. [8]Furthermore, the word of a friend or relative is not considered proof. [9]Moreover, the record must be legal and moral. [10]In fact, it is easier to get in this record book by beating an established record than by creating a new category or event. [11]Also, it helps to have the record reported in the news media. [12]Of course, affidavits signed by witnesses must accompany your request when you finally write for your claim to fame. [13]That is, if you manage to break an existing record.

Assignment 1:B

List all of the transition words in the passage below by sentence number. Then label each one according to the relationship between sentences (i.e., contrast, time, reason, etc.) which it shows.

DOLPHINS

[1]With their shiny, graceful, gray bodies, dolphins appear to be large fish. [2]Nevertheless, they are really warm-blooded mammals. [3]As a result, although they can dive as deep as a thousand feet and stay underwater for up to fifteen minutes at a time, dolphins, like whales, must surface to breathe air through a blowhole on top of their heads.

[4]Dolphins are social animals and love company. [5]Many of them, in fact, even enjoy being around humans. [6]It is not uncommon to hear of dolphins giving rides through the water to humans.

[7]In addition to being playful, dolphins are helpful to men. [8]For example, as early as 400 B.C. the Greek poet Arion was saved from drowning by a dolphin. [9]From then until now, dolphins have been helping swimmers who are in trouble. [10]Swimmers, however, are not the only humans they help. [11]In some parts of the world, they can be counted on to help men catch fish.

[12]Moreover, dolphins are very intelligent. [13]A dolphin's brain resembles a human brain, but it is larger. [14]Consequently, some people claim that dolphins are really smarter than men. [15]Of course, there is no way of proving this point. [16]Brain size is not an absolute measure of intelligence. [17]Furthermore, measuring dolphins' intelligence in other ways is not possible since men cannot fully communicate with them. [18]Apparently, however, dolphins communicate with each other. [19]At any rate, they make whistling, clicking, and buzzing sounds which seem to be at least a form of language. [20]So far, however, men have not been able to figure out the communication code the dolphins use. [21]Thus, no one really knows what they are thinking. [22]If we could communicate with dolphins, perhaps they could teach us to be as happy as they seem to be. [23]At least that is what some people think.

Assignment 1:C

List all of the transition words in the passage below by sentence number. Then label each one according to the relationship between sentences (i.e., contrast, time, reason, etc.) which it shows.

PUZZLES

[1]Occasionally, people do not enjoy active sports. [2]They do, however, like mental competition. [3]In these cases, puzzles are one pastime in which people can compete without an active opponent. [4]In the first place, anyone who has had a pleasant experience in solving pencil and paper games is more apt to try the sport again. [5]Furthermore, he may even be interested in trying more difficult games. [6]On the other hand, one who has not had success may possibly turn to another type of puzzle or may give up the sport altogether. [7]For years, puzzle magazines have been listing their crossword puzzles as easy, medium, or difficult. [8]As a result, a person who has not tried a crossword puzzle before may begin with an easy one and have success. [9]He may then try a harder puzzle and solve it. [10]Thus it is possible to become proficient in a very short time without becoming frustrated. [11]Soon the puzzle fan will be able to solve more challenging puzzles. [12]Eventually, even a puzzle labeled *challenger* will not stop him.

Assignment 1.1:A

Write the passage below, supplying the appropriate transition words. Make sure that the transition words you choose show the proper relationships between sentences.

AMERICAN INDIANS

It is often thought that the American Indians were all savages. _____ , it is easy to get this idea from

                                                   1

watching movies and television programs. Examining historical evidence, _____ , reveals a quite

     2

different picture. There were many different Indian tribes and types of Indians, and, _____ ,

     3

different Indians behaved in different ways.

        _____ , some Indian tribes seemed to be more civilized than the Europeans who came to

                4

America from across the Atlantic. _____ , there were other Indians whose civilizations were very

                                    5

primitive.

        A number of famous Indian tribes, _____ , were very warlike. Many other tribes,

                                              6

_____ , lived very peacefully and used weapons only for hunting food. Still others did not use

   7

weapons at all but were completely agricultural.

        _____ , anyone who makes sweeping generalizations about American Indians is making a

                8

big mistake.

Assignment 1.1:B

Write the passage below, supplying the appropriate transition words. Make sure that the transition words you choose show the proper relationship between sentences.

MEN AND FLIGHT

Many Americans believe that the Wright Brothers were the first men to fly. _____ , men had

                                                  1

ascended high into the sky over one hundred years before the Wright Brothers made their historic first flight.

        In 1783, the first successful hydrogen-filled balloon carried men aloft to an altitude of 3,000 feet for 45

minutes. _____ , French soldiers used balloons for military purposes. _____ , in

     2   3

1860, the world's first successful aerial photographs were made from a balloon flying over Boston.

_____ 4 , gas-filled balloons were used for observation of the enemy during the U.S. Civil War.

_____ 5 , hot air balloons were developed.

All of these airships, _____ 6 , flew because they were "lighter than air." _____ 7 , men, like the Wright Brothers, would develop machines which would fly even though they were heavier than air.

This development, _____ 8 , would have to wait until the necessary power sources were available.

_____ 9 , in the years before the twentieth century, balloons offered men the only means of flight.

Assignment 1.1:C

Write the passage below, supplying the appropriate transition words. Make sure that the transition words you choose show the proper relationships between sentences.

INDIAN CIVILIZATIONS

Some of the most advanced civilizations in the world developed in the pre-colombian South and Central America.

_____ 1 , early Spanish explorers expected to find a civilization inferior to the one they had left

behind in Europe. What they found in the new world, _____ 2 , surprised them. Even those who had

seen the greatest cities of Europe at that time marvelled at the grandeur of some of the new world cities.

Tenochtitlán, the capital of the Aztec empire (Mexico City today), surpassed all the others.

_____ 3 , the Spanish conquistadores took advantage of the facilities Tenochtitlán offered.

_____ 4 , when Cortez, the conqueror of Mexico, was wounded, he agreed to be treated by an Indian

doctor—he saw no need to send for a European physician. _____ 5 , he reported that the medical

care he had received was more than adequate by European standards.

_____ 6 , the Mayan civilization, which preceded the Aztec culture, was even more highly

developed in many ways. _____ 7 , by the time the Spanish arrived its glory had ceased to exist.

_____ 8 , no one really knows why the Mayan civilization declined.

2. VARIETY IN WRITING

Good writing demands variety in sentence length and combining/transforming methods. Some simple sentences should remain as they are while others should be combined by using different methods. When writing, do not overuse any one sentence combining or transforming method.

Assignment 2:A

Rewrite the sentences below into an acceptable paragraph (or paragraphs). Vary the length of your sentences and use a variety of transforming/combining methods. Where appropriate, use transition words.

EINSTEIN

Albert Einstein was born on March 14, 1879.

He was born in Ulm, Germany.

Albert Einstein's father was a small merchant and manufacturer.

He went to elementary school in Munich, Germany.

Later he went to school in Switzerland.

He was a physicist.

He advanced the theory of general relativity.

He is known throughout the world.

He was the most eminent scientist of this century.

Some claim he was the greatest scientist of all time.

His theories were very advanced.

He first advanced the theory that mass and energy are equivalent and interchangeable.

His astonishing theory of relativity has been verified by modern scientists.

The greatest proof of his theories has come since his death.

He opened the door to nuclear fission.

He received the Nobel Prize in 1921.

He disliked publicity and honors.

He helped form the Hebrew University.

The Hebrew University is in Jerusalem.

He spent his last twenty-two years at the Institute for Advanced Study.

The Institute for Advanced Study is in Princeton, New Jersey.

Albert Einstein died April 18, 1955.

Assignment 2:B

Rewrite the sentences below into an acceptable paragraph (or paragraphs). Vary the length of your sentences and use a variety of transforming/combining methods. Where appropriate, use transition words.

PRIMATES

Monkeys belong to the primate family.

Apes belong to the primate family.

The primate family is one of the major groups of mammals.

Primates nurse their young with milk.

The word "primate" comes from the Latin word *primus.*

Primus means "first."

Scientists classify men as primates.

Most primates live in tropical places.

Men live in almost all regions of the world.

Men live in almost all climates of the world.

A few primates live on the ground.

Most primates spend their time in trees.

Primates have good eyes.

Primates have grasping hands.

Primates have grasping feet.

Primates' bodies are well suited to life in the trees.

Primates have large eyes.

Primates' eyes look straight forward.

Higher primates can focus both eyes on the same object.

This ability helps them judge distances.

Some primates also see colors.

Many other mammals have claws.

Primates have flat nails on their fingers.

Primates have flat nails on their toes.

The nails help support enlarged pads.

The pads are on the ends of their fingers.

The pads are on the ends of their toes.

The pads are sensitive to touch.

The pads have nonskid ridges.

Most primates have large brains.

Primates are among the most intelligent of mammals.

Primates do not depend much on their sense of smell.

One part of their brain is relatively small.

This part is related to the sense of smell.

Primates have fewer young than most mammals.
A mother bears only one or two young at a time.
The young primates stay with their mothers for a longer period of time.
The longer period with their mothers allows the young primates to learn more.
Young primates learn from their mothers.
Young primates learn from the group they live in.

Assignment 2:C

Rewrite the sentences below into an acceptable paragraph (or paragraphs). Vary the length of your sentences and use a variety of transforming/combining methods. Where appropriate, use transition words.

CHESS

Chess is the most popular game in the world.
The kings lead the chess armies.
The kings face all kinds of dangerous situations.
Castles attack them.
Bishops attack them.
Knights attack them.
The knights are on horseback.
The king is trapped.
The king must surrender to the other army.
The game is over.
Every new game of chess is a different battle.
The two players are the generals.
The generals plan the battle.
Chess originated in India and Persia.
Chess originated more than 1300 years ago.
Chess is a "royal" game.
Chess provides challenge for adults.
Chess provides challenge for children.
Chess provides excitement for adults.
Chess provides excitement for children.
The word "chess" comes from a Persian word.
The Persian word is *shah.*
Shah means king.
"Checkmate" comes from an Arabic phrase.
The Arabic phrase is *shah mat.*
Shah mat means "the king is dead."
Chess is very popular in some countries.
Chess champions in these countries are famous.
Sports heroes are famous in other countries.
Chess is played by people all over the world.

Assignment 2.1:A

From the facts given below, write correct basic sentences. Then combine your sentences appropriately and write them in paragraph form. The result will be a short descriptive essay.

SCOUTING IN THE UNITED STATES

Members:

Boy Scouts
Cub Scouts: boys 8–11 years old
Boy Scouts: boys 12–14 years old
Explorer Scouts: boys 15+ years old or high school students

Girl Scouts
Brownies: girls 7–8 years old
Junior Girl Scouts: girls 9–11 years old
Cadette Girl Scouts: girls 12–14 years old
Senior Girl Scouts: girls 14–17 years old

Beginnings:

Boy Scouts
Founded by Lord Baden-Powell, England, 1908
Incorporated in the United States, 1910
National charter granted by U.S. Congress, 1916

Girl Scouts
Founded by Mrs. Juliette Gordon Low, Savannah, Georgia, 1912

Ranks:

Cub Scouts—bobcat, wolf, bear, lion, and webelo
Boy Scouts—tenderfoot, second-class, first-class, star, life, and eagle

Emphases:

Threefold development—mental, moral, and physical

Stresses:

Boy Scouts
Outdoor knowledge and skills, training in citizenship, manual arts, wood and camp craft, lifesaving, first aid, sports and games

Girl Scouts
Agriculture, arts and crafts, community life, health and safety, homemaking, international friendship, nature, sports and games

Publications:

Boy Scouts—*Boy's Life*
Girl Scouts—*American Girl*

Assignment 2.1:B

From the facts given below, write correct basic sentences. Then combine your sentences appropriately and write them in paragraph form. The result will be a short descriptive essay.

REPUBLIC OF IRELAND

Name: Republic of Ireland, *Éire* (in Gaelic)
Earlier names: Irish Free State (1922–1937) and Éire (1937–1949)
Capital: Dublin
Major cities: Dublin, Cork, Limerick, Galway, Waterford
Location: Island in eastern North Atlantic Ocean, near England
Area: 27,136 square miles
Highest point: Carrantuohill (3,414 feet above sea level)
Lowest point: coast (sea level)
Languages: Gaelic (Irish) and English
Religion: 94% Roman Catholic, Episcopalian 5%
Government: Republic
Head of State: President
Head of Government: Prime Minister
International Cooperation: United Nations (UN), Organization for Economic Cooperation and Development
    (OECD), Council of Europe
National Anthem: *Amhran na OhFiann* ("The Soldier's Song")
Economy:
    Agriculture—livestock, dairy products, wheat, barley, potatoes, turnips, sugar beets, and oats
    Industries and products—bread and biscuit making, brewing, textile milling, whiskey distilling, metal
        products, and paper
    Chief exports—live animals, foodstuffs, beverages, processed tobacco, textiles, and manufactured goods
    Chief imports—machinery and electrical goods, vehicles, iron and steel, coal and petroleum products
Monetary unit: Irish pound

Assignment 2.1:C

From the facts given below, write correct basic sentences. Then combine your sentences appropriately and write them in paragraph form. The result will be a short descriptive essay.

SHAKESPEARE

Name: William Shakespeare
Born: 1564, Stratford-on-Avon, England
Died: 1616, Stratford-on-Avon, England (age: 52)
Father: prosperous businessman and town mayor
Education: Latin grammar school
Married: 1582, to Anne Hathaway, a neighboring farm girl 8 years his senior
Children: three—Susanna, Hamnet, and Judith
Stage life:

     1592, successful actor in London

     1592–1594, London theaters closed because of plague, Shakespeare writes poetry

     1594, joins Chamberlain's Men, company of actors

     1599, Chamberlain's Men build Globe theater

     1603, King James comes to throne, Chamberlain's Men become the King's Men

     1610, Shakespeare retires from stage

Major types of plays and examples of each:

Comedies	Histories	Tragedies	Romances
The Comedy of Errors	Henry VI (3 parts)	Romeo and Juliet	The Winter's Tale
The Taming of the Shrew	Richard III	Julius Caesar	The Tempest
Much Ado about Nothing	Richad II	Hamlet	Cymbeline
As You Like It	Henry IV (2 parts)	Othello	Pericles, Prince of Tyre
	Henry V	Macbeth	
	Henry VIII	Antony and Cleopatra	

Total number of plays written: 36

Assignment 2.2:A

From the facts given below, write correct basic sentences. Then combine your sentences appropriately and write them in paragraph form. The result will be a short process (history) essay.

MAJOR EARTHQUAKES

Date		Place	Deaths	Magnitude*
526	May 20	Syria, Antioch	250,000	N.A.
1268	– – – –	Asia Minor, Cilicia	60,000	N.A.
1290	Sept. 27	China, Chihli	100,000	N.A.
1556	Jan. 24	China, Shaanxi	830,000	N.A.
1730	Dec. 30	Japan, Hokkaido	137,000	N.A.
1737	Oct. 11	India, Calcutta	300,000	N.A.
1755	Nov. 1	Portugal, Lisbon	60,000	8.75**
1908	Dec. 28	Italy, Messina	83,000	7.5
1920	Dec. 16	China, Gansu	100,000	8.6
1923	Sept. 1	Japan, Tokyo	99,330	8.3
1927	May 22	China, Nan-Shan	200,000	8.3
1970	May 31	Northern Peru	66,794	7.7
1976	Feb. 4	Guatemala	22,778	7.5
1976	July 23	China, Tangshan	655,235	8.2
1978	Sept. 16	Northeast Iran	25,000	7.7

*Magnitude of earthquakes is measured on the Richter scale. Each higher number represents a tenfold increase in energy measured in ground motion. N.A. indicates that information on the magnitude is not available.

**Magnitude has been estimated from earthquake intensity.

Assignment 2.2:B

From the facts given below, write correct basic sentences. Then combine your sentences appropriately and write them in paragraph form. The result will be a short process (history) essay.

MAN'S JOURNEY TO THE MOON

Date	Crew	Mission Name	Orbits	Duration	Remarks
4/12/61	Gagarin	Vostok 1	1	1h 48m	First manned orbital flight
5/5/61	Shepard	Mercury-Redstone 3	*	15m 22s	First American in space
8/6–7/61	Titov	Vostok 2	16	25h 18m	First space flight of more than 24 hours
2/20/62	Glenn	Mercury-Atlas 6	3	4h 55m 23s	First American in orbit
8/11–15/62	Nikolayev	Vostok 3	64	94h 22m	Vostok 3 and 4 made first group flight
8/12–15/62	Popovich	Vostok 4	48	70h 57m	Came within 3 miles of Vostok 3
6/16–19/63	Tereshkova	Vostok 6	58	70h 50m	First woman in space
10/12/64	Komarov, Feoktistov, & Yegorov	Voskhod 1	16	24h 17m	First 3-man orbital flight; first without space suits
3/13/65	Belyayev & Leonov	Voskhod 2	17	26h 02m	Leonov made first "space walk" (10 min.)
3/23/65	Grissom & Young	Gemini-Titan 3	3	4h 53m 00s	First manned spacecraft to change its orbital path
12/15–16/65	Schirra & Stafford	Gemini-Titan 6-A	16	25h 51m 24s	Completed world's first space rendezvous with Gemini 7
12/21–27/68	Borman, Lovell, & Anders	Apollo-Saturn 8	10**	147h 00m 42s	First flight to moon; views of lunar surface televised to earth
3/3–13/69	McDivitt, Scott, & Schweickart	Apollo-Saturn 9	151	241h 00m 54s	First manned flight of lunar module
5/13–26/69	Stafford, Cernan, & Young	Apollo-Saturn 10	31**	192h 03m 23s	First lunar module orbit of moon
7/16–24/69	Armstrong, Aldrin, & Collins	Apollo-Saturn 11	30**	195h 18m 35s	First lunar landing made by Armstrong & Aldrin; collected soil, rock samples; lunar stay time 21h, 36m, 21s

*suborbital
**moon orbits

Assignment 2.2:C

From the facts given below, write correct basic sentences. Then combine your sentences appropriately and write them in paragraph form. The result will be a short process (history) essay.

INVENTIONS AND INVENTORS

Invention	Inventor	Date	Place
Paper	Tsai Lun	about 50 A.D.	China
Windmill	unknown	about 650 A.D.	Persia
Magnetic compass	unknown	about 1150 A.D.	China
Printing with movable type	Johann Gutenberg	about 1440	Germany
Microscope	uncertain (probably Zacharias Janssen)	about 1590	Netherlands
Thermometer	Galileo Galilei	1593	Italy
Balloon	Montgolfier Brothers	1783	France
Electric battery	Alessandro Volta	1800	Italy
Bicycle	K. MacMillan	1840	Scotland
Safety match	Gustaf Erik Pasch	1844	Sweden
Safety pin	Walter Hunt	1849	U.S.A.
Elevator	Elisha G. Otis	1853	U.S.A.
Zipper	W. L. Judson	1896	U.S.A.
Jet engine	Frank Whittle	1936	England
Helicopter	Igor Sikorsky	1939	U.S.A.

Assignment 2.3:A

From the facts given below, write correct basic sentences. Then combine your sentences appropriately and write them in paragraph form. The result will be a short comparison/contrast essay.

MAJOR LAKES OF THE WORLD

Name	Continent	Area (square miles)	Length (miles)	Depth (feet)	Elevation (feet)
Caspian Sea	Asia-Europe	143,550	760	3,360	–92
Lake Superior	North America	31,700	350	1,333	600
Lake Victoria	Africa	26,828	250	270	3,720
Aral Sea	Asia	25,300	280	223	174
Lake Huron	North America	23,100	206	750	579
Lake Michigan	North America	22,300	307	923	579
Lake Tanganyika	Africa	12,700	420	4,708	2,534
Lake Baykal	Asia	12,162	192	1,464	1,493
Great Bear Lake	North America	12,028	395	5,315	512
Lake Nyasa	Africa	11,430	360	2,226	1,550
Great Slave Lake	North America	11,031	298	2,015	513
Lake Erie	North America	9,910	241	210	570
Lake Winnipeg	North America	9,417	266	60	713
Lake Ontario	North America	7,550	193	802	245
Lake Ladoga	Europe	6,835	124	738	13

Note: A lake is a body of water surrounded by land. Although some lakes are called seas, they are lakes by definition.

Assignment 2.3:B

From the facts given below, write correct basic sentences. Then combine your sentences appropriately and write them in paragraph form. The result will be a short comparison/contrast essay.

THE CONTINENTS OF THE WORLD

Name	Area (square miles)	Percent of earth	Population (estimated)	Percent of world population	Annual rate of population growth
Asia	16,988,000	29.5	2,559,200,000	59.2	2.3%
Africa	11,506,000	20.0	457,000,000	10.6	2.4%
North America	9,390,000	16.3	363,000,000	8.4	1.6%
South America	6,795,000	11.8	234,000,000	5.4	2.8%
Europe	3,745,000	6.5	685,800,000	15.9	1.3%
Australia	2,968,000	5.2	14,400,000	0.3	1.2%
Antarctica	5,500,000	9.6	----	----	----

Assignment 2.3:C

From the facts given below, write correct basic sentences. Then combine your sentences appropriately and write them in paragraph form. The result will be a short comparison/contrast essay.

AVERAGE TEMPERATURES AROUND THE WORLD

Place	January	April	July	October
Copenhagen, Denmark	32	42	62	48
Paris, France	37	50	66	52
Rome, Italy	44	58	77	62
Cairo, Egypt	56	70	83	75
Cape Town, South Africa	70	63	55	62
Hong Kong	60	71	83	77
Tokyo, Japan	39	55	76	62
Bangkok, Thailand	80	87	84	83
Sydney, Australia	72	61	53	64
Rio de Janeiro, Brazil	78	77	69	72
Buenos Aires, Argentina	74	63	50	60
Mexico City, Mexico	54	65	64	60

APPENDIX A
FORMS OF CONTENT WORDS

Parentheses indicate words rarely, if ever, used.

NOUN	VERB	ADJECTIVE	ADVERB
ability	enable	able	ably
absence	absent	absent	absently
achievement	achieve	achievable	--------
acquisition	acquire	(acquisitive)	(acquisitively)
act, activity, action	act	active	actively
adequacy	--------	adequate	adequately
admission	admit	admissible	admissibly
advantage	--------	advantageous	advantageously
adventure	adventure	adventurous	adventurously
advice	advise	advisory	(advisorily)
aggression, aggressor	aggress	aggressive	aggressively
allowance	allow	allowable	(allowably)
ambition	--------	ambitious	ambitiously
appreciation	appreciate	appreciative	appreciatively
appropriation	appropriate	appropriate	appropriately
approximation	approximate	approximate	approximately
attention	attend (to)	attentive	attentively
attraction	attract	attractive	attractively
authority	authorize	authoritative	authoritatively
basis	base	basic	basically
benefit	benefit	beneficial	beneficially
bravery	brave	brave	bravely
breadth	broaden	broad	broadly
brilliance	--------	brilliant	brilliantly
capability	--------	capable	capably
capture, captor	capture	captive	(captively)
center	centralize	central	centrally
circle	circle	circular	(circularly)
clarity	clarify	clear	clearly
cleverness	--------	clever	cleverly
comfort	comfort	comfortable	comfortably
competition	compete	competitive	competitively
complex	--------	complex	complexly
comprehension	comprehend	comprehensive	comprehensively

NOUN	VERB	ADJECTIVE	ADVERB
computer	compute	--------	--------
compulsion	compel	compulsive	compulsively
confidence	confide (in)	confident	confidently
consideration	consider	considerable	considerably
construction	construct	constructive	constructively
consumption	consume	consumable	--------
conversion	convert	convertible	(convertibly)
correction, correctness, corrector	correct	correct	correctly
corruption	corrupt	corrupt	(corruptly)
courage	encourage	courageous	courageously
crime, criminal, criminality	--------	criminal	criminally
culture	--------	cultural	culturally
curiosity	--------	curious	curiously
danger	endanger	dangerous	dangerously
defense	defend	defensive	defensively
definition	define	definitive	(definitively)
delinquency	--------	delinquent	(delinquently)
dependence, dependent	depend (on)	dependent	dependently
description	describe	descriptive	descriptively
desire	desire	desirable	desirably
destruction	destroy	destructive	destructively
determination	determine	determinable	--------
difference	differ (from)	different	differently
disadvantage	--------	disadvantageous	(disadvantageously)
disaster	--------	disastrous	disastrously
disgrace	disgrace	disgraceful	disgracefully
displeasure	displease	--------	--------
division	divide	divisible	(divisibly)
domination	dominate	dominant	dominantly
doubt	doubt	doubtful	doubtfully, doubtlessly
eagerness	--------	eager	eagerly
education	educate	educational	educationally
effect	effect	effective	effectively
emotion	emote	emotional	emotionally
endurance	endure	endurable	(endurably)
energy	energize	energetic	energetically
enforcement	enforce	enforceable	(enforceably)
enthusiasm	enthuse	enthusiastic	enthusiastically
equality	equalize	equal	equally
erection	erect	erect	(erectly)
essence, essential	--------	essential	essentially
example	exemplify	exemplary	(exemplarily)
excellence	excel	excellent	excellently
exhaustion	exhaust	exhaustive	exhaustively
expansion, expanse	expand	expansive	expansively
exploitation	exploit	exploitable	(exploitably)
extension	extend	extensive	extensively
fame	--------	famous	famously
familiarity	familiarize	familiar	familiarly
fatality	--------	fatal	fatally
favor	favor	favorite	--------
fertility, fertilizer	fertilize	fertile	(fertilely)
firmness	firm	firm	firmly
force	force	forceful	forcefully
foreigner	--------	foreign	(foreignly)

NOUN	VERB	ADJECTIVE	ADVERB
frankness	--------	frank	frankly
friend, friendliness	befriend	friendly	friendly
gallantry	--------	gallant	gallantly
government	govern	governmental	(governmentally)
gradualness	--------	gradual	gradually
grievance	grieve	grievous	grievously
harshness	(harshen)	harsh	harshly
haste	hasten	hasty	hastily
hero, heroism	--------	heroic	heroically
ignorance	ignore	ignorant	ignorantly
imagination	imagine	imaginative	imaginatively
immediacy	--------	immediate	immediately
immensity	--------	immense	immensely
impression	impress	impressive	impressively
impossibility	--------	impossible	impossibly
independence	--------	independent	independently
indication	indicate	indicative	(indicatively)
individual, individualism, individuality	individualize	individual(istic)	individually
inevitability	--------	inevitable	inevitably
influence	influence	influential	influentially
insecurity	--------	insecure	insecurely
inspiration	inspire	inspirational	inspirationally
intelligence	--------	intelligent	intelligently
legality	legalize	legal	legally
legislation, legislator, legislature	legislate	legislative	(legislatively)
liberality, liberalization	liberalize	liberal	liberally
liberty, liberation	liberate	--------	--------
limitation	limit	(limitable)	(limitably)
location	locate	local	locally
looseness	loosen	loose	loosely
loyalty	--------	loyal	loyally
magnet	magnetize	magnetic	(magnetically)
might	--------	mighty	mightily
minimum	minimize	minimal	minimally
movement	move	movable	--------
negation	negate	negative	negatively
notice	notice	noticeable	noticeably
obligation	obligate	obligatory	(obligatorily)
observation, observer	observe	observant	observantly
occasion	occasion	occasional	occasionally
occupation	occupy	occupational	(occupationally)
offense, offender	offend	offensive	offensively
opportunity, opportunist	--------	opportune	opportunely
opposition, opposite	oppose	opposite	(oppositely)
oppression, oppressor	oppress	oppressive	oppressively
optimism, optimist	--------	optimistic	optimistically
part	part	partial	partially
permission, permit	permit	permissive	permissively
perpetuation	perpetuate	perpetual	perpetually
person, personality	personalize	personal	personally
persuasion	persuade	persuasive	persuasively
politics (always pl.), politician	--------	political	politically

NOUN	VERB	ADJECTIVE	ADVERB
possession, possessor	possess	possessive	possessively
poverty	impoverish	poor	poorly
prediction	predict	predictable	predictably
preparation	prepare	preparatory	--------
prevention	prevent	preventive	(preventively)
profit	profit	profitable	profitably
prohibition	prohibit	prohibitive	prohibitively
provision	provide	provisional	provisionally
recurrence	recur	recurrent	recurrently
regularity	regularize	regular	regularly
regulation	regulate	regulatory (regulative)	(regulatively)
relation, relative	relate	relative	relatively
reliance, reliability	rely (on)	reliable	reliably
remedy	remedy	remedial	(remedially)
reminiscence	reminisce	reminiscent	(reminiscently)
respect	respect	respectful, respective	respectfully, respectively
response	respond	responsive	responsively
responsibility	--------	responsible	responsibly
resistance	resist	resistant	(resistantly)
restriction	restrict	restrictive	(restrictively)
rivalry, rival	rival	rival	--------
satisfaction	satisfy	satisfactory	satisfactorily
scorn	scorn	scornful	scornfully
secrecy	--------	secretive	secretively
section	sectionalize, section	sectional	(sectionally)
sentiment, sentimentality	--------	sentimental	sentimentally
separation	separate	separate	separately
significance	signify	significant	significantly
skill	--------	skillful	skillfully
solemnity	solemnize	solemn	solemnly
steadiness	steady	steady	steadily
strangeness	--------	strange	strangely
student	study	studious	studiously
subsidiary, subsidy	subsidize	subsidiary	--------
success	succeed	successful	successfully
suddenness	--------	sudden	suddenly
suitability	suit	suitable	suitably
suspicion, suspect	suspect	suspicious	suspiciously
swiftness	--------	swift	swiftly
symbol	symbolize	symbolic	symbolically
sympathy	sympathize	sympathetic	sympathetically
system	systematize	systematic	systematically
technique	--------	technical	technically
(temporariness)	(temporize)	temporary	temporarily
tightness	tighten	tight	tightly
toleration	tolerate	tolerable	tolerably
transfer, (transference)	transfer	transferable	--------
treachery	--------	treacherous	treacherously
triumph	triumph (over)	triumphant	triumphantly
tyranny, tyrant	tyrannize	tyrannical	(tyrannically)
uncertainty	--------	uncertain	uncertainly
victory, victor	--------	victorious	victoriously
vigor	invigorate	vigorous	vigorously
virtue	--------	virtuous	virtuously
vitality	vitalize	vital	vitally
violence	--------	violent	violently

APPENDIX B
SOME COMMON NONCOUNT NOUNS AND UNIT EXPRESSIONS

advice (piece, bit)

anger (fit, pique)

beef (piece, slice, side, pound, kilo, serving, platter, helping, can, tin)

beer* (bottle, glass, mug, can, vat, keg)

biology**

catsup (bottle, dab, teaspoon, cup)

chalk (piece, box)

chemistry**

cloth* (yard, bolt, meter, piece, scrap, sample)

cocoa (cup, mug, glass, teaspoon, can, serving)

concrete (yard, bag, wheelbarrow)

corn* (ear, field, bushel, can, kernel)

economics**

entertainment (night, hour)

fabric* (yard, meter, bolt, piece, scrap, sample)

film* (roll, box, package, can, reel)

flour (sack, bag, pound, cup)

fog* (day)

food* (plate, serving, mouthful)

furniture (piece, room, set)

glass* (piece, pane, sheet)

gold (ounce, bar, bag)

grass (field, clump, blade)

gravy (bowl, boat, ladle, pan, serving)

hair* (strand, head, handful)

homework (page)

honey (jar, can, comb, pound)

intelligence (grain, ounce, lick [colloquial])

iron* (ton, pound, truckload, piece)

jealousy (fit, pique, attack)

juice (glass, pitcher, cup, quart, gallon)

junk (piece, pile, truckload)

lamb* (leg, slice, piece, pound, kilo, shoulder)

leather (piece, strip, square inch)

lemonade* (glass, pitcher, cup, quart, gallon)

lettuce (head, leaf)

luggage (piece, set)

lumber (piece, board foot, truckload)

mail (piece, bag, shipment)

material (see *fabric*)

mathematics**

meat (pound, kilo, serving, slice, platter, bite, helping)

medicine* (dose, teaspoon, drop) [also**]

pepper (spoon, pinch, dash)

photography**

pork (serving, slice, roast, loin, side, helping, pound, kilo, platter)

powder (box, can, keg)

pride (ounce)

rain* (inch, drop)

ribbon* (inch, foot, yard, piece)

rice (grain, cup, pound, bag, sack)

salt (spoon, pinch)

sand (grain, bucket, yard)

sight*/***

silver (ounce, bar, bag)

sleet

smell*/***

snow* (inch, foot, ton)

soup (bowl, tureen, ladle, spoonful, can, tin, pot)

stationery (box, ream)

stew* (bowl, tureen, ladle, spoonful, can, tin, pot)

stuff (box, room, pile, load)

sugar (sack, bag, pound, cup, spoon)

tin* (sheet, piece, square inch)

toast* (piece, slice)

toothpaste (tube, tin)

touch*/***

vision*/***

wheat (ton, ear, pound, bag, grain)

wind* (gust)

wine* (bottle, carafe, glass, drop)

wood (cord, piece, load)

work (unit, hour, day, piece, lick [colloquial])

* These nouns are normally noncount, but they can also be count nouns. When they are count nouns, the meaning is different from the noncount meaning (see p. 10 in *Sentence Construction*).

** These are areas of study. Unit expressions are not normally used with them. However, unit expressions (area, branch, course, unit, page) relating to courses, books, etc., are sometimes used with them.

*** Senses do not normally use unit expressions.

APPENDIX C
IRREGULAR VERB FORMS

	TIMELESS			TIME-INCLUDED	
				Present	Past
Base	*d-t-n*	*-ing*	*-s* form	No-*s* Form	
be	been	being	is	am, are	was, were
bear	borne, born	bearing	bears	bear	born
beat	beaten, beat	beating	beats	beat	beat
become	become	becoming	becomes	become	became
begin	begun	beginning	begins	begin	began
bend	bent	bending	bends	bend	bent
bet	bet	betting	bets	bet	bet
bite	bitten, bit	biting	bites	bite	bit
bleed	bled	bleeding	bleeds	bleed	bled
blow	blown	blowing	blows	blow	blew
break	broken	breaking	breaks	break	broke
bring	brought	bringing	brings	bring	brought
build	built	building	builds	build	built
burst	burst	bursting	bursts	burst	burst
buy	bought	buying	buys	buy	bought
catch	caught	catching	catches	catch	caught
choose	chosen	choosing	chooses	choose	chose
come	come	coming	comes	come	came
cost	cost	costing	costs	cost	cost
creep	crept	creeping	creeps	creep	crept
cut	cut	cutting	cuts	cut	cut
deal	dealt	dealing	deals	deal	dealt
dig	dug	digging	digs	dig	dug
dive	dived	diving	dives	dive	dived, dove
do	done	doing	does	do	did
draw	drawn	drawing	draws	draw	drew
drink	drunk	drinking	drinks	drink	drank
drive	driven	driving	drives	drive	drove
eat	eaten	eating	eats	eat	ate

	TIMELESS			TIME-INCLUDED	
				Present	Past
Base	d-t-n	-ing	-s form	No-s Form	
fall	fallen	falling	falls	fall	fell
feel	felt	feeling	feels	feel	felt
fight	fought	fighting	fights	fight	fought
find	found	finding	finds	find	found
flee	fled	fleeing	flees	flee	fled
fly	flown	flying	flies	fly	flew
forget	forgotten	forgetting	forgets	forget	forgot
forgive	forgiven	forgiving	forgives	forgive	forgave
freeze	frozen	freezing	freezes	freeze	froze
get	got, gotten	getting	gets	get	got
give	given	giving	gives	give	gave
go	gone	going	goes	go	went
grow	grown	growing	grows	grow	grew
hang	hung	hanging	hangs	hang	hung
hang(a person)	hung	hanging	hangs	hang	hanged
have	had	having	has	have	had
hear	heard	hearing	hears	hear	heard
hide	hidden	hiding	hides	hide	hid
hit	hit	hitting	hits	hit	hit
hold	held	holding	holds	hold	held
hurt	hurt	hurting	hurts	hurt	hurt
keep	kept	keeping	keeps	keep	kept
kneel	knelt, kneeled	kneeling	kneels	kneel	knelt, kneeled
know	known	knowing	knows	know	knew
lay	laid	laying	lays	lay	laid
lead	led	leading	leads	lead	led
leave	left	leaving	leaves	leave	left
lend	lent	lending	lends	lend	lent
let	let	letting	lets	let	let
lie (recline)	lain	lying	lies	lie	lay
lie (tell an untruth)	lied	lying	lies	lie	lied
light	lighted, lit	lighting	lights	light	lighted, lit
lose	lost	losing	loses	lose	lost
make	made	making	makes	make	made
mean	meant	meaning	means	mean	meant
meet	met	meeting	meets	meet	met
pay	paid	paying	pays	pay	paid
put	put	putting	puts	put	put
quit	quit	quitting	quits	quit	quit
read	read	reading	reads	read	read
ride	ridden	riding	rides	ride	rode
ring	rung	ringing	rings	ring	rang
rise	risen	rising	rises	rise	rose
run	run	running	runs	run	ran

	TIMELESS		TIME-INCLUDED		
				Present	Past
Base	d-t-n	-ing	-s form	No-s Form	
say	said	saying	says	say	said
see	seen	seeing	sees	see	saw
seek	sought	seeking	seeks	seek	sought
sell	sold	selling	sells	sell	sold
send	sent	sending	sends	send	sent
set	set	setting	sets	set	set
shake	shaken	shaking	shakes	shake	shook
shine (shoes)	shined	shining	shines	shine	shined
shine (sun)	shone	shining	shines	shine	shone
shoot	shot	shooting	shoots	shoot	shot
shrink	shrunk	shrinking	shrinks	shrink	shrank
shut	shut	shutting	shuts	shut	shut
sing	sung	singing	sings	sing	sang
sink	sunk	sinking	sinks	sink	sank
sit	sat	sitting	sits	sit	sat
slay	slain	slaying	slays	slay	slew
sleep	slept	sleeping	sleeps	sleep	slept
wake	waked, woken	waking	wakes	wake	waked, woke
wear	worn	wearing	wears	wear	wore
weave	woven	weaving	weaves	weave	wove
weep	wept	weeping	weeps	weep	weapt
win	won	winning	wins	win	won
wind	wound	winding	winds	wind	wound
wring	wrung	wringing	wrings	wring	wrung
write	written	writing	writes	write	wrote

APPENDIX D
SOME COMMON TWO-WORD VERBS

INSEPARABLE

call on = ask to recite
come back = return
come over = visit
get up = arise
get along = progress
get along with = be friendly, cooperate
get out of = escape, evade
get through = finish
get by = succeed with little effort
get over = recover
go on = happen
go over = review
keep on = continue
look into = investigate
look for = seek
look like = resemble
look out = beware
make out = succeed
make sure of = verify
run over = hit with a car
run out of = exhaust
run across = discover (by chance)
run into = meet (by chance)
show up = appear

SEPARABLE

back up = move to the rear
call up = telephone
do over = repeat
fill out = complete
give back = return
give up = cease, surrender
hand in = submit
hand out = distribute
keep up = maintain
leave out = omit
let go = release
look up = search for
look over = examine
make up = prepare, invent, compensate
make (one's mind) up = decide
pick out = choose
pick up = lift, raise
put away = return to proper place
put off = postpone
put (clothing) on = dress
put out = extinguish
put up = raise
show off = display
take off = remove, undress
take up = introduce, discuss
take down = record in writing

APPENDIX E
VERBS WHICH MAY BE FOLLOWED BY NOUN PHRASES

Followed by -*ing* forms only	Followed by *to* + base form only	Followed by either form
admit	agree	afford
allow	appear	attempt
appreciate	ask	begin
avoid	beg	continue
can't help	care	go
consider	decide	like
deny	deserve	prefer
enjoy	endeavor	remember
escape	expect	start
finish	forget	stop
get through	hope	try
insist on	intend	
imagine	learn	
keep on	mean	
make	need	
mind	plan	
miss	promise	
plan on	want	
postpone	wish	
practice		
resent		
resist		
stop		
study		
suggest		